de Gruyter Studies in Organization 18

Hardy: Strategies for Retrenchment and Turnaround

de Gruyter Studies in Organization

An international series by internationally known authors presenting current fields of research in organization.

Organizing and organizations are substantial pre-requisites for the viability and future developments of society. Their study and comprehension are indispensable to the quality of human life. Therefore, the series aims to:

- offer to the specialist work material in form of the most important and current problems, methods and results;
- give interested readers access to different subject areas:
- provide aids for decisions on contemporary problems and stimulate ideas.

The series will include monographs, collections of contributed papers, and handbooks.

Cynthia Hardy

Strategies for Retrenchment and Turnaround: the Politics of Survival

W DE G

Walter de Gruyter · Berlin · New York 1990

Cynthia Hardy
Associate Professor of Policy at the Faculty of Management, McGill University, Montréal, Québec, Canada

Library of Congress Cataloging-in-Publication Data

Hardy, Cynthia, 1956–
Strategies for retrenchment and turnaround : the politics of survival / Cynthia Hardy.
(De Gruyter studies in organization ; 18)
Includes bibliographical references
ISBN 0-89925-598-1 (U.S. : alk. paper)
1. Corporate turnarounds--Management. I. Title. II. Title: Retrenchment. III. Series
HD58.8.H634 1989
658.4′063--dc20

Deutsche Bibliothek Cataloging in Publication Data

Hardy, Cynthia:
Strategies for retrenchment and turnaround: the politics of survival / Cynthia Hardy. – Berlin ; New York : de Gruyter, 1989
(De Gruyter studies in organization ; 18)
ISBN 3-11-011612-X
NE: GT

♾ Printed on acid free paper

Typesetting: Arthur Collignon GmbH, Berlin. – Printing: Gerike GmbH, Berlin. – Binding: Dieter Mikolai, Berlin. – Cover design: Johannes Rother, Berlin.

IN THIS DAY AND AGE, LAYOFFS AND OUTRIGHT FIRINGS ARE ODIOUS AND DISTASTEFUL.
SO WE HERE AT CONSOLIDATED PHILIFLAXTERS INC. DECIDED TO DO SOMETHING ABOUT IT...
NOW WE CALL THE WHOLE PROCEDURE 'CREATIVE DOWNSIZING.'
AISLIN '85
MONTREAL GAZETTE

Acknowledgements

I would like to acknowledge the support of the Social Sciences and Humanities Research Council of Canada. I also owe my thanks to the participants in this study, who generously gave me their time, cooperation and insights. Finally, thanks to Dave and Ray for sensible suggestions and sound support.

Contents

Introduction

This book is about strategies for retrenchment and turnaround. Retrenchment refers to activities that reduce the scope or scale of an organization's operations. It is usually provoked by an environment that is declining in some sense – in terms of markets, revenues, funding, etc. – precipitated by such factors as increased competition, demographics, or government policies. Retrenchment activities include plant (or factory) closure, voluntary or enforced dismissals (also known as severance, layoffs, and terminations), reduced working hours, work-sharing, etc. Academics and managers have used a number of different labels to describe retrenchment, including downsizing, resizing, cutbacks, and rationalization, among others. Chapter 11 and the glossary provide more information about these terms.

Whichever terminology is used, retrenchment has been, and will continue to be, one of the major challenges facing contemporary managers. In the business world, increasing economic uncertainty and fierce foreign competition are making retrenchment decisions imperative for organizational competitiveness and success. Public sector managers have, in many countries, had to contend with restrictions in government funding, which have forced them to reduce the scale of their operations.

Such retrenchment activities cannot be disassociated from turnaround. Turnaround strategies are designed to restore the health and viability of the enterprise following a period of decline. Retrenchment and turnaround are, therefore, often linked, since cutbacks are usually part of an overall plan to improve organizational performance. Many organizations are phasing out only part of their operations in order to protect the larger entity. One factory may be closed while others continue to operate; some people lose their jobs, but others stay on, responsible for seeing the organization through a critical period. Retrenchment must, in these circumstances, be considered as an investment in survival. Contraction is the price paid for future viability and, as such, deserves the same creative analysis as any other investment decision; otherwise downgrading, not downsizing, will be the result. Retrenchment is not, then, purely the disbanding of operations; sustaining the larger organization is equally important.

Long-term survival depends on the commitment and motivation of the continuing employees. Unfortunately, the personnel reductions involved in these decisions can lead to resentment, fear, union hostility, industrial action, and unfavourable publicity. Given the problems that led to the need for cutbacks in the first place, management can ill afford to allow productivity to fall, strikes to occur, unfavourable publicity to deter customers, or people with much needed skills to leave. Managers have, nevertheless, often ignored these human implications of downsizing, because they fail to see the link between them and the survival of the enterprise. Such attitudes, thus, reflect a short-sighted business perspective.

Many of the adverse effects of retrenchment – for both employees and organizational survival – can be avoided with a retrenchment program that takes into account the needs of both the departing and the continuing employees, as well as the unions and other interest groups which are involved. It will allay many of the fears associated with the cutbacks, and help employees to view retrenchment as a challenge rather than a threat, enabling them to respond positively to the changes demanded of them. If an organization is to achieve a satisfactory turnaround, individuals need to be convinced that retrenchment is a step towards increased profitability and efficiency; that there are opportunities associated with a more streamlined operation; that their increased effort will be rewarded; and that their concerns will be taken care of.

The impact of retrenchment on employees highlights its political dimension. It is a contentious issue which results in numerous interest groups, both inside and outside the organization, trying to intervene in the retrenchment process. Managers, if they are to be successful, must learn to accommodate these political pressures – they cannot approach retrenchment as a purely economic phenomenon. Retrenchment is thus an illuminating arena in which to view political strategies because of the conflict over scarce resources. It is not, however, the only situation in which managers find themselves faced with competing interest groups – the long-term survival of organizations in many different circumstances depends on the effective management of politics. The specific example of retrenchment thus provides a useful springboard for the examination of these broader pressures, showing that management in general is often both an economic and a political problem.

Drawing on research carried out in nine organizations in Canada and Britain since 1978, this book shows how retrenchment can be managed to accommodate both economic and political pressures. The first chapter provides the broad framework for the book. It discusses in more detail the economic and political pressures that beset managers during retrenchment. Part I discusses how the organizations dealt with these demands. They are divided into three groups: those that focussed on managing the various interest groups (chapters 2–4); those that had to balance economic and political concerns (chapters 5–9); and one organization that ignored political issues (chapter 10). These chapters provide detailed information on how individual organizations dealt with their problems and how successful they were. A table, which summarizes their main characteristics, is provided in the introduction to Part I. The findings from these organizations, which span both public and private sectors, and range from multinationals to health authorities, are then discussed and elaborated in Part II. It provides a series of lessons and recommendations in terms of both choosing a strategy and implementing it (chapters 11–12). In the final chapters (13 and 14), the political aspects of retrenchment are explored more closely and used to develop a broader framework for managers who have to deal with competing interest groups in order to survive.

Chapter 1: The Political and Economic Pressures of Retrenchment

Retrenchment is a strategy that is employed primarily in response to economic pressures. For reasons such as declining markets and government funding cuts, cost cutting is called for, which often involves the reduction of personnel. Because of these problems, which precipitated the need for retrenchment, attention is focussed on these economic demands, rather than on the needs of individual employees. Managers are, as a result, often concerned with finding ways to close plants, save costs, and remove overhead as rapidly as possible (Price & D'Aunno, 1983). They often wish to maintain as much control over the process as possible – orchestrating who leaves and when, and keeping those with critical skills in the organization. Employers facing these difficulties are often reluctant to institute policies to deal with the human dimension of retrenchment. With factories being closed, jobs phased out, and departments cut back, they may be unwilling to spend time and money on individuals who will shortly cease to be employees.

Simply to cite the moral duty of organizations to care for the well-being of their personnel in unlikely to convince employers to change their behaviour: such altruistic values are low on the list of priorities when financial concerns become pressing constraints. Employers will need to be convinced that ignoring employees and other interest groups and stakeholders can have a detrimental effect on the future of the firm. The fact is, however, that many organizations facing retrenchment are not going out of business completely; they are cutting back in some areas to protect the viability of the enterprise as a whole. Consequently, *survival* is as important as *retrenchment*, and retrenchment must be considered as part of a turnaround strategy.

Survival will depend on the cooperation of the various interest groups affected by the cutbacks. For example, turnaround hinges on the continued commitment of the employees who remain (Bibeault, 1982).

These individuals are required to be productive and creative even though they have seen the jobs of their colleagues disappear, and may face an uncertain future themselves. Morale will be fragile, and unlikely to withstand many unsympathetic or insensitive actions on the part of management (Greenhalgh, 1983; Luce, 1983). Continuing employees quickly become aware of how their peers have been dismissed. If they perceive them to be victims of unfair practices, morale and commitment suffers, which translates into an exodus of employees as soon as economic conditions permit. Recruiting problems will arise as prospective candidates learn of the company's record (Morin & Yorks, 1982; Stybel, 1978).

Union resistance also has to be taken into consideration. Factory occupations have occurred in Britain where workers have attempted to prevent closure or to win better conditions by delaying plans, impeding the sale of assets, interfering with the transfer of production, and generating media and public disapproval (Clarke, 1979; Hardy, 1985 a, b; Hemmingway & Keyser, 1975). Union disapproval can also take the form of strikes, difficult contract negotiations, noncooperation, and political initiatives (Gordus et al., 1981).

Finally, the organization has to consider its public image. Unfavourable publicity concerning cutbacks can provoke political intervention or leave customers, community leaders, and union representatives worried about the future of the organization. If these groups try to prevent or influence the retrenchment program, managers will find their task considerably more complicated. Organizations which violate their social responsibilities may face legal action (Eves, 1985; Lehr & Middlebrooks, 1984).

The successful management of retrenchment thus has a political dimension. Managers must ensure that stakeholders – interest groups with a stake in the outcome of the retrenchment strategy –, such as continuing and departing employees, unions, the media, and politicians, are not alienated by the downsizing program. Ignoring them because of a preoccupation with saving money in the short term will translate into long-term costs and inhibit recovery. Demoralized employees, alienated unions, government intervention, and unfavourable publicity all make the implementation of cutbacks more difficult and more expensive. Since retrenchment is the key to survival, managers by ignoring the political implications will be compromising the future of the enterprise.

Balancing Economic and Political Pressures

It is clear, then, that retrenchment – and turnaround – contain both economic and political components. The former relates to managing efficiency and effective task allocation (Wamsley & Zald, 1973). In the context of retrenchment, it means that costs have to be cut, budgets reduced, and productivity raised – sometimes in significant proportions and in a short time frame. Some organizations need to maintain strict control over the downsizing process if liquidity is a problem or scarce skills have to be protected. Managers must accommodate these economic needs if the organization is to survive and prosper. The political component refers to the ability to manage conflict and generate commitment (Wamsley & Zald, 1973). In other words, retrenchment is also a "people" problem if, for example, there is a risk of union resistance, political intervention, or if future survival depends on the continued commitment and loyalty of continuing employees. Managers will, then, have to accommodate these stakeholders, creating commitment to their plans and resolving conflict, if they are to successfully implement retrenchment and turnaround strategies.

Political and economic pressures can affect the organization in a number of ways (Hardy, 1986 a). In some cases, economic problems will be highly constraining. In other words, some managers will find their freedom of action severely circumscribed by a lack of resources or because large cutbacks have to be implemented immediately. Other organizations may have considerably more economic freedom in the form of cash reserves, time, and other resources. Managers may also be constrained by political pressures in the sense that their ability to carry out retrenchment depends on the cooperation of internal and/or external interest groups, which have the power to disrupt their plans. *Diagram 1* illustrates these pressures.

[1] represents a situation in which political issues are important, while economic concerns are less constraining. It might be typical of a large company which, while needing to rationalize operations, has sufficient resources to be able to circumvent short-term pressures. Since operations are continuing in other parts of the company, relations with employees and other interest groups are particularly important. The employer cannot expect continuing employees to provide the necessary motivation and productivity if they have seen their ex-colleagues badly treated. Managers may also be vulnerable to union action, adverse

Diagram 1: The Economic and Political Pressures of Retrenchment

		Economic Pressures	
		Unimportant	Important
Political Pressures	Important	[1]	[2]
	Unimportant	[4]	[3]

publicity, or political intervention. Strong unions can easily disrupt operations, including cutbacks or a rundown. Publicity that casts doubt on the viability of the enterprise will shake fragile customer confidence, causing them to seek other sources of supply, thereby worsening the effects of decline and making turnaround even more difficult. Organizations dependent on public funding, engaged in government contracts, or subject to government regulations may find themselves held hostage to the political agendas of national or local politicians who wish to avoid large-scale layoffs or factory closures in key constituencies. The absence of immediate economic constraints means that there is sufficient time and money to conduct a gradual reduction or provide support for those leaving the company, thereby accommodating the concerns of stakeholders and mitigating some of these political pressures.

[2] reflects the situation in which managers must reconcile both economic and political considerations. For reasons such as those given above, it is important to maintain high levels of commitment and cooperation among internal and external interest groups. At the same time, however, the company is constrained by cost and control factors. For example, the competitive and financial situation may be so bad that action must be taken immediately, with little money available to cushion the blow for those individuals affected; or future success may depend on maintaining people with critical skills in the organization.

[3] managers in this cell consider political issues to be unimportant to future success, leaving them free to pursue economic goals. Such a

situation may characterize a company which is going out of business completely. The pressure of bankruptcy makes short-term needs paramount in managers' eyes, while the complete discontinuance of operations makes the maintainance of effective employee relations appear largely irrelevant. In this situation, managers would also consider themselves immune to intervention by other interest groups.

[4] represents the case where management is constrained by neither issue. This is a relatively unlikely occurrence, although it may characterize some "asset stripping" and divestment decisions of large conglomerates. If the entire business is being divested, there is little pressure on management to accommodate employees, and if the divestment is occurring solely to make an immediate financial gain (as opposed to restoring competitiveness and profitability), short-term pressures would be minimal.

Of particular interest are cells [1] and [2] in which managers have defined political pressures as crucial to the success of the downsizing exercise. In effect, these managers have made the link between retrenchment and turnaround. They have recognized the need to accommodate the various stakeholders in order to implement effective strategies and safeguard the survival of their organization. Managers who pay attention to employee needs for ethical reasons also belong here. These cells require a more critical appraisal of retrenchment methods – cuts cannot be made solely on the basis of economic criteria; their impact on employees and other groups must be taken into consideration. As a result, the choice of retrenchment strategy becomes problematic.

Managers in the remaining two cells have explicitly or implicitly decided that political pressures are irrelevant. They may be making an accurate assessment of their situation – it is conceivable that, in certain circumstances, the cooperation of employees or goodwill of unions, government, and other groups has no bearing on success. What is also possible, however, is that managers have *incorrectly* dismissed political pressures, believing that they can ignore stakeholders with no detriment to their plans whereas, in reality, they are jeopardizing the successful implementation of their plans and organizational survival. It has been argued above that managers often undervalue the importance of the human dimension of retrenchment to organizational success; in which case, it can be argued that a common error is for managers to categorize themselves in cells [3] or [4] when, in fact, they belong in [1] or [2].

Summary and Conclusions

Retrenchment often involves the need to balance political and economic pressures, if the continued viability of the organization is to be guaranteed. Pure economics would appear to dictate the simple announcement of those to be terminated on a notice board – effective forthwith with no or minimal severance pay. Political pressures, on the other hand, would suggest that managers provide advance notice, embark on measures to reduce the number of terminations, and offer voluntary severance supported by a number of measures to help employees find new jobs. The following chapters examine how a number of different organizations dealt with these conflicting demands (*diagram 2*).

These organizations, for the most part, consisted of managers who felt that retrenchment had a political dimension, and maintaining favourable relations with the various stakeholders was an important part of the process. It was not simply for humanistic or altruistic reasons, but because they were aware that the continued success of their enterprises depended upon effective employee relations, and the absence of intervention from outside constituencies. The following chapters describe the actions that they took and some of the problems they ran into. They show that retrenchment strategies can be chosen

Diagram 2: Economic and Political Pressures: The Organizations

Political Pressures	*Economic Pressures*: Unimportant	*Economic Pressures*: Important
Important	ICI CIL Whitefields [1]	Andersons Midville AECL Air Canada [2] Ville Marie
Unimportant	[4]	[3] Northville

to balance economic and political pressures – to make cuts quickly and effectively and to protect the human resource element.

The organizations have been divided into three groups (see *diagram 2*). Three of the organizations chose to focus on *managing the interest groups*. They deemed the political aspects of retrenchment to be important and were relatively unconstrained by short-term economic pressures. Another five organizations had to *balance economic and political pressures* in that they had to reconcile short-term cost and control constraints with a need to accommodate employees and other groups. Finally, the case study of an organization that chose to *ignore political pressures* is presented. In this example, managers mistakenly believed that political issues were unimportant. When they acted on this assumption, they alienated a variety of stakeholders who were able to prevent them from implementing their plans. Part I discusses these case studies in more detail.

Ideally, the study would also encompass organizations that illustrate all four cells. As every researcher is well aware, however, research work is rarely an ideal, but a compromise with time, money, and other commitments. The inclusion of other organizations proved beyond the scope of this particular study. The omission should not detract from the book's main objective of learning more about the political dimension of retrenchment and turnaround, although fuller exploration of these different categories may well prove to be a fruitful area for future research.

Part I: The Organizations

Introduction

The following chapters describe nine organizations which experienced retrenchment in a variety of forms, ranging from early retirement programs to factory closures. They include private manufacturing firms, state-owned enterprises, health authorities, and a social service centre. They span both public and private sectors in Canada and Britain. (The British organizations have also been described in Hardy, 1985 a.) A number of different strategies and support mechanisms were used by the managers concerned to address both the organizational and the individual issues associated with the cutbacks. The following chapters provide the reader with the opportunity to obtain a deeper insight into the problems and circumstances facing each individual organization, and the actions taken in response to them. A table summarizing their main characteristics is provided below (*Table 1*).

For the most part these organizations have dealt with retrenchment effectively. This "over-representation" of successful organizations should not cause any surprise: retrenchment is a sensitive issue to which many managers are reluctant to allow research access, particularly when things have not gone as well as they might. As such, the studies provide an opportunity to learn how retrenchment can be successfully managed. This is not to say that the organizations did not make some mistakes. Moreover, Chapter 10 documents the failure to close a hospital. These stumbling blocks illustrate some of the things *not* to do.

Interviews were conducted with managers, employees, union representatives, and other interest groups in each of the organizations. In total, some 200 people were interviewed. Documentary evidence was analyzed, including managerial and union reports, memoranda, press releases and articles, and statistical data. At the request of managers, the names of four of the organizations have been changed to guarantee anonymity. The names of all individuals and some of the locations have also been disguised. For more details on the methodology, please see Appendix V.

Summary of Organizations

Managing the Interest Groups

Imperial Chemical Industries (ICI)

ICI is a British divisionalized, multinational chemical manufacturer. In 1975, it had sales of £3,129 million and 195,000 employees worldwide, including 129,000 in the UK. That year, ICI announced the closure of a plant with more than 1,000 employees in the north west of England. It was to take place between 1975 and 1980, with a gradual rundown that would allow the transfer of production to other manufacturing sites. The reason for the closure was a plan to reduce the number of manufacturing sites in the division in order to compete more effectively with European producers. The company was worried about the possibility of resistance from its blue-collar workers, who were represented by national unions. It also wanted to avoid a high media profile. The closure was carried out according to schedule and without union resistance. 1975 had seen a fall in profits, but results improved during the late 1970s. The company experienced more severe problems when 1980 saw the first loss since the 1930s. It initiated more retrenchment measures. UK employment had fallen to 84,000 in 1980; it fell another twenty percent to 62,000 in 1983, as company profitability was restored (Cooke, 1987).

CIL

CIL is a Canadian chemical manufacturer which, in 1982, had sales of $1,060 million and 7,000 employees. In response to declining performance – a fall in net earnings by two thirds –, the company announced a series of cost cutting measures in 1982. They included the partial closure of an explosives plant, involving 176 individuals, in an isolated Ontario community. Managers were anxious to avoid alienating the union because of the risk of sabotage, forthcoming contract negotiations, and the fact that part of the operation would continue to operate. They were also anxious to avoid bad publicity, especially since the closure of a subsidiary had previously attracted considerable criticism for ignoring the needs of its employees. The closure was successfully carried out in 1983, and performance figures for that year and the following year improved. 1985 brought about more problems as net income fell again, and a loss was recorded in 1986. The remaining part of the plant was closed during 1985.

Whitefields

Whitefields is a nonunionized, multinational organization. Canadian operations involve more than 11,000 people and a turnover of more $ 2 billion. In 1982, employees were offered an early retirement package, in an attempt to cut overhead costs in 1983. The company ensured that the program was completely voluntary in order to avoid compromising its policy on job security. 432 individuals, out of the 1,288 eligible employees, took advantage of the offer.

Balancing Economic and Political Pressures

Andersons

Andersons is a North American multinational which, in 1978, employed nearly 60,000 individuals. In response to losses of $ 200 million in 1978 and high debt, Andersons announced the closure of a Scottish engineering factory. It employed some 1,500 employees, many of whom were represented by national unions. The area was famous for resistance to factory closures during the early 1970s, and industrial relations at this factory had been problematic with a number of strikes and lockouts. Managers were, as a result, concerned about union resistance. They took a series of steps to save jobs. Ultimately, they helped to set up a small subcontracting firm on the original site, which provided jobs for 200 employees. While the factory was closed successfully from a managerial perspective, the company continued to experience severe problems. Losses were recorded every year between 1980 and 1984. The number of employees fell to 20,000 in 1985.

Atomic Energy of Canada Ltd (AECL)

AECL is a government-owned company in the nuclear power business. In 1982, nearly 8,000 people worked for the company. In response to falling orders, AECL instituted a 25 per cent cut in its workforce of 2,500 in manufacturing operations, which involved 500 employees being selected for dismissal. A voluntary severance program was taken up by another 80 employees. Cutbacks in the larger organization were also carried out as net income fell in 1984 and 1985. Managers were highly sensitive to political and public opinion and, as a result, wanted to ensure that the retrenchment program went ahead smoothly. The layoffs were carried out, although some grievances were instituted against the company by both union and nonunion employees.

Air Canada

Air Canada is a state-owned airline which employs more than 22,000 people and supplies flights throughout the world. 1982 saw a $ 40 million profit turn into a $ 32 million loss, and initiated a series of retrenchment measures. Air Canada offered a voluntary severance program to all its nonunionized, managerial staff, of which some 18 per cent – some 600 individuals – took advantage. Much like AECL, Air Canada is sensitive to public opinion and political intervention. The program was carried out without major problems, although the global retrenchment strategy has met with mixed success. Profits were recorded in 1983 and 1984, but 1985, once again, saw a loss.

Ville Marie

Ville Marie is a government-funded social service centre in Montreal, Quebec which employed around 650 individuals. In 1981, a cut in government funding reduced its budget by 11 per cent – $ 2 million. Ville Marie tried to resist the budget cut but to no avail. It then implemented the cutback which caused the loss of 22 jobs and some tense relations with the unions, which were eventually resolved.

Midville

Midville is an area health authority in Britain's National Health Service. Area managers closed a hospital during the late 1970s, in response to financial restrictions which were resulting in an estimated deficit of £ 1 million. Managers were highly sensitive to public opinion, union resistance, and government intervention. They took steps to accommodate these stakeholders and, as a result, were able to close the hospital.

Table 1: Main Characteristies of the Organizations

	ICI	CIL	Whitefields
Size of Organization (# Employees)	195,000 worldwide in 1975	7,000 in 1982	11,000 in Canada in 1982
Retrenchment Program	factory closure	partial factory closure	early retirement program
Timing	1976–80	1983	1983
# Employees	1000	176	432
Unionized	yes	yes	no
Financial Situation	fall in profits in 1975	fall in profits in 1982	net earnings decreasing
Managerial Concerns: Economic	not considered constraining	not considered constraining	not considered constraining
Managerial Concerns: Political	primarily resistance from blue-collar workers	union resistance, publicity	no compromise of full employment practice
Advance Warning	yes	yes	yes
Joint Committees	yes	yes	not applicable
Voluntary Severance	yes	yes	yes
Conditions on Severance	no	no	no
Compensation	yes	yes	yes
Outplacement	yes	yes	not applicable
Outcome of Retrenchment	carried out successfully	carried out successfully	carried out successfully
Organizational Performance	improved in short term, worsened in 1980 which led to more retrenchment measures as profits were restored	improved in 1983 and 1984, loss in 1986	net earnings increase until 1985, fall in 1986

Table 1: Continued

	Andersons	AECL	Air Canada
Size of Organization (# Employees)	58,000 in 1978	8,000 in 1982	23,000 in 1982
Retrenchment Program	factory closure	25 per cent cut in operations staff	voluntary severance for managers
Timing	1978–80	1983	1983
# Employees	1500	600	600
Unionized	yes	yes	no
Financial Situation	large loss in 1978	fall in orders	loss in 1982
Managerial Concerns: Economic	loss and debt	cost of layoffs, loss of key skills	loss of key skills
Managerial Concerns: Political	resistance from workforce	public and political concern	public and political concern
Advance Warning	not before initial announcement	yes	yes
Joint Committees	yes	yes	no
Voluntary Severance	no	not at first	yes
Conditions on Severance	not applicable	individuals selected	yes
Compensation	yes	yes	yes
Outplacement	yes	yes	no
Outcome of Retrenchment	carried out successfully	carried out successfully	carried out successfully
Organizational Performance	profit in 1979 losses 1980–4	profits fell in 1984, 1985	profits in 1983, 1984, loss in 1985

Table 1: Continued

	Ville Marie	Midville	Northville
Size of Organization (# Employees)	650 in 1981	4,500 in district in 1978	11,000 in district in 1978
Retrenchment Program	11 per cent budget cut	hospital closure	hospital closure
Timing	1981	1977–9	1977–8
# Employees	22 lost jobs	70 in hospital	90 in hospital
Unionized	yes	yes	yes
Financial Situation	cut in government funding of 11 per cent	£ 1 million budget deficit	£ 1 million budget deficit
Managerial Concerns: Economic	balancing budget	reducing expenditures	reducing expenditures
Managerial Concerns: Political	first resisting cutbacks, later employee relations	union resistance	none
Advance Warning	yes	yes	yes
Joint Committees	yes	no	no
Voluntary Severance	no	yes or choice of similar job	not applicable
Conditions on Severance	selection by seniority	no	not applicable
Compensation	not applicable	yes	not applicable
Outplacement	no	within AHA	not applicable
Outcome of Retrenchment	some tensions with union	carried out successfully	closure not implemented
Organizational Performance	budget balanced	expenditures reduced	continuing financial and political problems

Ignoring Political Pressures

Northville

Northville is an area health authority in the north of England. In 1977, managers attempted to close a maternity hospital due to an overprovision of maternity beds and a budget deficit of £1 million. They failed because they did not predict the resistance from employees, doctors, unions, and patient representatives that resulted in their closure recommendation being overturned. The decision cost the health authority half a million pounds a year, at a time of considerable financial restraint.

I.1 Managing the Interest Groups

Chapter 2: Imperial Chemical Industries

This chapter concerns the closure of a factory in the northwest of England. The factory, known here as "Mountside" works, was a production site in one of the divisions of a large British multinational, Imperial Chemical Industries (ICI).

Mountside works was situated in a large city, on a site adjoining the divisional headquarters. The factory manufactured a large number of chemical products, most of which were intermediaries sold to other sites in the division and outside the company. Chemicals had been manufactured there in one form or another for one hundred years, and the company had been involved for over fifty years.

In 1975, the divisional chairman announced that Mountside works had a life expectancy of only five to ten years. This decision can be traced to a number of events. The divisions had been reorganized in 1971, and the nylon business, previously a highly profitable part of division, had been moved elsewhere. The removal of this successful business revealed the difficulties being experienced in the remainder of the division when profits began to fall. European chemical manufacturers were working from a small number of highly complex integrated sites. The division's ten production sites required rationalization. Mountside was not a strong candidate for survival – it was situated in a residential area and wedged in between divisional headquarters and a hospital, with little room for expansion; and the plant was outdated. There were other large integrated sites in the division which, in the eyes of one senior manager, were the "obvious places to concentrate production".

Following this announcement, management embarked on the construction of a closure plan to detail how the numerous products and businesses should be run down. Alongside this was a "people plan" which stated how many people would be needed, with which skills, and for how long. A five-year rundown helped to respond to both business and people needs. The former required the transfer of certain products to other sites where new equipment and facilities had to be built. Until these transfers were complete, it was important for Mountside to maintain production and accommodate customer demand. Employee needs warranted the gradual release of more than 1,000 employees, allowing attrition and turnover to reduce the need for redundancies. Task forces were established to ascertain individual needs, key personnel, and communication and retraining requirements during the rundown process.

A year later, a second announcement stated that Mountside works would close by the end of 1980. A presentation was made of the reasons for closure and details of the rundown to managers, supervisors, shop stewards, and elected representatives who, in turn, passed the information on to the workforce. Local union officials were informed by letter, and later invited to a similar presentation, in June 1976.

After this presentation, the local officials passed the matter up to their national officials[1] to see if anything could be done to prevent the closure. This was the normal procedure: if "failure to agree" occurred at the local level, the matter was passed up the negotiating hierarchy. In November 1976, local officials reported that their national officers were satisfied with the company's reasons for the closure. Consequently, they intended to play no part in local negotiations, which would be left to the shop stewards "to get the best deal they could for their members". The stewards could call them back in if they were unable to agree with management on any particular issue.

The closure proceeded according to plan, with the works closing completely in 1980 and only two individual grievances occurring. These were referred to the industrial tribunal for unfair dismissal and resolved by the arbitration officer; otherwise all disagreements were resolved at the local level, between stewards and management. The rundown schedule was adhered to, with no industrial action. Productivity remained stable; the number of customer complaints fell, as well as the percentage of those complaints which were considered justified; and absenteeism declined.

---

[1] The main unions were the National Union of General and Municipal Workers (NUGMW) and the Amalgamated Union of Engineering Workers (AUEW). Also involved were the Electrical, Electronic, Telecommunications, and Plumbing Union (EETPU), the Union of Construction, Allied Trades, and Technicians (UCATT) and the Boilermakers Union.

Another indicator of the success can be gauged from employees' comments. The general feeling was that while the closure was "sad" and a "shame", it was well managed and in no way could any criticism be attached to the company.

> The closure was well-managed (redeployed staff employee).
>
> I have no criticisms of the way the closure was handled (general worker).
>
> I could never call the company. I was pleased with the way it was done (ex-manual worker).
>
> It's marvellous how it's been done. Every help one could imagine was there (redeployed manual worker).

It would appear, then, that ICI was justified in concluding that:

> the rundown of the works was a successful endeavour from both the business and people viewpoints (managerial report).

The Process

To account for this success, we need to take a closer look at the process used to implement the closure. It had started many years before, when a new works manager had been appointed in 1971. He knew that "in all probability, my job was going to be to close those works". It was considered important that this closure should be handled carefully. Management wished to avoid any local opposition which could spread to other factories, either through the divisional shop stewards' committee or as a result of intervention by local union officials. Divisional management made it "very clear" that nothing should happen at Mountside which could escalate and affect the division as a whole or the carefully scheduled transfer of production.

> We had considered the possibility of an outright strike. That could have been quite damaging at that point because we had large chunks of the division's business, some of it perhaps not very profitable but nevertheless important, and important from the customer's point of view (manager).

The anticipation of further closures also prompted managers to act carefully. With national unions involved, managers were reluctant to do anything which would set a bad precedent for decisions taken elsewhere in the company and make it difficult to implement future cutbacks. ICI did not consider it to be in its own interests to handle change in a way that alienated the rest of the company's population. The onus was on local management to manage the closure in a "reasonable way".

To prepare for the closure, the new works manager began to introduce a more consultative and open style of decision making. This was in direct contrast with the "work oriented, authoritarian and cost conscious" regime that preceded him, but it was in keeping with similar changes that were occurring elsewhere in the company. The culture change involved bringing together the managers, stewards, and supervisors (who were particularly demoralized as a result of the new working responsibilities). Residential courses were arranged for these groups in 1974 and 1975. It was considered essential to improve relations between management and unions if the closure was to be implemented without resistance.

> I just can't see how we would have tackled the closure successfully in the old culture (works manager).

Once this groundwork was established, the closure became a reality and consultation was extended to focus on it. By mid-1976, a Redeployment Steering Group (RSG) had been set up, chaired by a Head of Department (HoD) who had been made responsible for redeployment, and with the personnel manager, assistant personnel manager, three craft stewards, and three general worker stewards as members. The steering group was a problem-solving group, not a negotiating body. Its aim was to identify problems and make recommendations to the works manager, who would then take the final decision. It was intended to involve the stewards and to address employees' needs during the rundown. This committee was considered to be an integral part of a successful strategy.

> It can be concluded that the RSG was a massive time-wasting activity since many of the procedures it developed were little used, some convoluted arguments came to nothing in the end; nevertheless it was a very useful safety valve. It allowed the works manager to stand back from the fray and act as the final arbiter and as the years rolled on what was achieved was a remarkable degree of trust on both sides. This prevented any real industrial unrest occurring or the need to resort to the formal negotiating procedure (managerial report).

The steering group involved manual workers; the staff situation was somewhat different. Members of staff were dealt with on a more individual basis and representatives were only involved if specifically asked for. A similar group for staff was set up but not until 1978, and it lasted less than a year, due to the fact that staff were new to unionization (only the Association of Scientific, Technical, and Managerial Staff (ASTMS) had official recognition). Representatives were inexperienced, and staff members were ambivalent regarding union involvement, often preferring a more personalized approach.

Communication was another important aspect of the closure process. In addition to the information passed on by managers and stewards, a weekly bulletin was established. It was available in newsheet form and via the internal phone. The information was updated weekly, and the bulletin ran for more than two years.

Considerable efforts were made to help with outplacement. Retraining schemes were paid for by the company in, for example, heavy goods and public service vehicle driving. A "job shop" was set up displaying vacancies. The company advertised on behalf of its workers and contacted firms which might be interested in hiring. Forty per cent of workers were redeployed within the company. Follow-ups on successful redeployments were posted in the job shop to encourage other workers who might be interested in moving. Paid time off for interviews was available, and employees were provided with help on interview and job search techniques.

ICI tried to reassure people that they would not be thrown out of their jobs. A statement on job security made in January 1975 promised that enforced redundancy would occur only as a last resort.

> I really did feel that without that statement we would have had such initial reation because the assumption would be that people were just going to be thrown out (manager).

Both employees and union officials were satisfied that people "wouldn't be turned out onto the street".

Job security was complemented by the provision of generous redundancy terms of two to three times the state minimum, and by payment in lieu of notice. The redundancy payments were worked out on the basis of age and service. The predominantly old and long-serving workforce (40 per cent were over the age of 46 and more than 50 per cent had more than 10 years service) qualified for large sums of money. These terms tempted many people to take voluntary severance.

> I am very conscious of the fact that the company's severance terms are so good that you really are bribing people to leave, and they couldn't resist the bribery (works manager).

While more than 80 per cent of employees indicated in 1975 that they wanted to stay with the company, less than 40 per cent actually did so.

The advance notice minimized the negative effects of job losses: attrition accounted for 16 per cent of the reductions; outplacement had a chance to work; managers could locate redeployment opportunities; the labour force was released gradually. The negative effects of a long rundown were avoided.

> Considering the long drawn-out and wearing process of closing a works down bit-by-bit over five years, morale and sense of humour within the works were maintained at a surprisingly good level (managerial report).

The Environment

Various environmental factors helped ICI in its bid to carry out a successful closure. First, the existence of relatively nonmilitant attitudes among local union officials helped to ensure that, although all manual workers were members of national unions, there was no official support for any resistance.

> It was told to us in no uncertain terms by the union officers that due to environmental problems and the age of the plant that it had to close. We were told then that there was nothing more we could do except get the best possible terms for the employees (steward).

It effectively robbed the shop stewards of much of their power.

> If the union officials were like that what chance did we stand? (steward).

There was also a reluctance among the members to take industrial action. They had rarely engaged in strikes or other forms of action.

> People don't want to go outside the gates [on strike]. They don't even want to lose overtime (steward).

Management had, however, helped to encourage these attitudes with a non-confrontational industrial relations policy. The culture change and consultation contributed to a climate of cooperation. The generous redundancy compensation dissuaded members from taking action.

> You can't put up a fight when the members wouldn't be with you. A lot of members would say "What the hell's it got to do with you – you're stopping me from getting my redundancy pay" (union official).

A second factor concerned the location and timing of the closure. The company was fortunate in closing a plant in an area with low unemployment. Local unemployment rates were under 7 per cent at that time, about the same as the national average. As a result, union officials and employees alike perceived few problems in finding other jobs, believing that there were "plenty of jobs outside".

> You've got to remember that the climate is totally different today [in 1980]. We had no unemployment then, or very little. Certainly as craft unions we had no major problem (local union officer).

A final factor which worked to management's advantage concerned the justification of the closure. The company appeared to have good reasons for closing Mountside. These were not, however, the "real" reasons – the need for a rationalization of manufacturing sites. Employees tended to focus on two environmental reasons – the close proximity of a potentially dangerous chemical works to a hospital and residential area, and the old age of the plant.

> Everything was explained and it was found to be sensible, such as the hospital right on the perimeter of the works. When it was explained about the environmental problems, to even think about putting chemical products here wasn't common-sense (steward).
>
> We had ideas about the closure a long time ago because of the environment of the place – we're near a hospital. We know that we couldn't get any more sanctions for putting new buildings up and putting more investment in because of the position of the works and also the place itself. Some of the sheds were so antiquated, you'd have to rip the whole place out and start from scratch (steward).

Despite the works manager's initial presentation of the need for the rationalization in terms of the division as a whole, other managers tended to convey the impression that the plant was closing because it was old, and because it was a dangerous site for a chemical works.

> [They] put around that we were closing Mountside works because of the environment – it was a nice easy explanation (works manager).

Because of this situation, and the fact that these environmental "reasons" were simple and visible, "most people tended to latch on to the environment bit of the argument – but it was only part of it and secondary" (manager).

Summary and Conclusions

ICI was very successful in its closure of Mountside works. This success can be attritubed to a number of factors. Management was aware of how damaging a badly managed closure could be in terms of provoking industrial action, harming employee relations, and jeopardizing other closures. In order to protect the company against these threats, managers devised a strategy that would safeguard employee needs during the closure, reassuring union officials and employees alike that there was nothing to fear. Extensive consultation and communication, outplacement aid, advance notice, voluntary severance, and generous redundancy compensation were provided. Environmental factors worked to ICI's advantage, and management was adept in exploiting them. As a result, ICI was able to implement the closure without mishap.

ICI has not always been so successful: in the mid-1970s the closure of a Scottish factory – "Brookside" – provoked resistance. Union leaders involved politicians and the press in an attempt to prevent it. Complaints were rife concerning the lack of consultation and communication, previous mismanagement, and uncertainty about what was happening. This was despite the fact that everyone was guaranteed jobs in another plant at the site.

The company conducted a study into the issue to try and find out what had caused the resistance. The findings revealed a number of problems. First, there had been a highly authoritarian culture at the plant, in which consultation and communication had not been encouraged. This situation had been exacerbated when the factory had been taken over from another division in the early 1970s. The new managers had initiated a series of changes in working relationships which had been implemented with insufficient communication. The result was "an accumulation of fear and suspicion". Second, the announcement of the closure, in March 1975, had come as a shock to employees since it had been preceded by three highly optimistic forecasts in December 1974, and January and February 1975. Moreover, the closure was to be put into effect very quickly, with work in one part of the plant finishing by June 1975, and the remainder in early 1976. A third problem concerned ineffectual relationships between local management and stewards. They had previously revolved around two people – the works manager and the senior steward. When these two individuals moved on – one through illness, the other through promotion – the entire basis of industrial relations at the plant was changed, and communication between the two sides became problematic.

Brookside represents quite a different picture to Mountside. The news of the closure did not come as a shock – although employees said that they did not believe the initial announcement; they could, in fact, trace the causes back to the 1950s and 1960s, and felt that the decision was a logical one. The lack of communication at Brookside had already created a climate of distrust which was not helped by the management of the closure itself. At Mountside, in contrast, consultation had been extended prior to the closure and was continued during it. The years leading up to the closure had seen the increased participation of the stewards and more openness on the part of management. The key actors at Mountside – the works manager and the senior steward of the National Union of General and Municipal Workers (NUGMW) – remained in their positions throughout nearly all of the rundown period.

As was mentioned at the beginning of this chapter, the Mountside closure was one of many that the company carried out. These closures represented a realignment of the company's business which began in the late 1970s and intensified in the 1980s, in response to a £48 million loss in 1980, the first since the 1930s, and a fall in the ratio of trading profit to sales from 15 per cent in 1974 to 6 per cent in 1980. These difficulties and the appointment of a new chief executive officer in 1982 prompted significant changes in the organization and, in particular, a relocation of production outside of the UK. These changes involved the acquisition of new markets, replacement of management, and the introduction of new structures, operating systems, roles, relationships, and culture. In the UK, a policy of rationalization reduced UK personnel by over 50 per cent between 1975 and 1983, and by one quarter between 1980 and 1983 alone. Business outside the UK and Western Europe increased from 40 per cent in 1974 to 52 per cent in 1984. The result has been an increase in profits – by 55 per cent between 1984 and 1985 – and an improvement in ROE from 11 to 9 per cent. (See Cooke, 1987 and Pettigrew, 1985 for more details).

Chapter 3: CIL Industries Ltd

CIL is a Canadian manufacturer and distributor of chemical and allied products. Established in 1862 as the Hamilton Powder Company, the enterprise has grown and diversified. Sales in 1982 were \$1,059.8 million, and the company was involved in more than six major businesses.

The recession left its mark on CIL during the early 1980s. Sales in 1982 were down from \$1,149.9 million the previous year, income from operations fell by nearly one-half (from \$111.2 million to \$61.7 million), and net earnings dropped by more than two-thirds (\$54.3 million to \$15.2 million). Earnings per share subsequently fell from \$4.69 in 1981 to \$0.82 in 1983 (figures from the 1982 Annual Report).

> In 1982 the Canadian economy experienced the worst recession since the 1930's ... The industries we supply experienced severe reduction in demand, leading to fierce competition for business at less than adequate prices. Costs of services and raw materials, and particularly of energy, continued to rise, creating a severe squeeze on profit margins (1982 Annual Report, p. 2).

As a result, a series of cost-reducing measures was employed in different parts of the company.

> The company took a number of actions during the year designed to reduce or constrain employment costs. It was necessary to reduce total employment by 16% through both permanent and temporary layoffs. A number of plants worked periods of reduced hours and participated in the federal government's unemployment insurance work-sharing program. Temporary changes were also made in vacation and overtime rules. A decision was made late in the year to maintain 1982 salary ranges throughout 1983 and these ranges were judged adequate to maintain competitiveness in the current environment (1982 Annual Report, p. 17).

These measures included the partial closure of the Nobel plant (explosives division) in October 1983, with which this chapter is concerned.

The production of nitroglycerine-based (NG) explosives was phased out involving the termination of 123 jobs, while the production of cap sensitive slurry (CSS) explosives was continued with 53 employees.

The Process

The plans for the partial closure were announced on June 7th, 1983. Falling orders had threatened at least one of two plants (the Nobel plant in Parry Sound, Ontario and the Beloeil plant, Quebec) for a number of years. This issue had been discussed with the unions[1] during contract negotiations, so the idea was not new to them. Eventually the choice of Nobel was made because it was an older plant and the cost of renovating it higher.

On the day following the announcement, a team consisting of four counsellors from head office was sent to the plant. Its function was to provide answers to any questions raised by the employees concerning the closure and the benefits for which they would qualify.

> [The aim was] to get as much information to all employees as quickly as possible so people had what they needed to make their own assessment right from the beginning (manager).

In addition to providing practical information, these individuals also helped to manage the inevitable trauma experienced by the employees who would be losing their jobs.

> It's very important when you make this [kind of] announcement ... that you move in and manage it (manager).

This counselling helped to offset the negative information with something more positive – it counteracted the news of the closure with details about the options open to employees, the benefits for which they would qualify, and the redundancy compensation which they would be paid. It minimized unanswered questions and uncertainty, and it had a symbolic impact; it showed employees that the company was prepared to spend time and money on them.

Another feature of the closure was the provision of five months notice. This time helped employees adjust and find new jobs. Managers felt

[1] The predominant union at Nobel was the United Steel Workers of America (USWA).

that it was essential for psychological adjustment and for the practical planning of such issues as vacations, purchases, new jobs, schooling, etc.

> I think it gave them [the employees] every possible advantage. From our point of view, I don't think it was negative (manager).

Four placement committees were established for unionized and staff employees with both employee and company representation. Their aim was to:

> find alternative employment for all affected employees, to determine retraining possibilities, to administer the counselling programs for employees, to keep employees informed of plans and activities undertaken (company report).

Union representatives were selected by the union president. Staff and company representatives were chosen by the plant manager. These committees decided who would get retraining, how the search for new jobs could be improved, and for which benefits and allowances people qualified. Their function was to involve the employees and the union in the rundown process, and to provide concrete outplacement aid. The company's view, however, was that the closure decision had been taken. It did not view the committees as vehicles whereby the union or employees could negotiate the closure itself.

> The aim was not to give them any role at all in making the major decisions about who goes, how do we shut it down, how is the money shared, but to give them some control of the details [surrounding the overall shutdown process] (manager).

Despite these restricted terms of reference, the dialogue between the union and management that was developed in the committees did enable them to work together more effectively.

> It worked well because what it did was keep the company and the union working together, solving the problems. By making them participants I think it was much more successful (manager).

A variety of support measures were developed. Employees received pay for time spent in interviews, general sessions, and seminars. They were granted three days off with pay plus meal and travel allowances to attend confirmed off-site interviews (42 employees took advantage of this). Fifteen employees received allowances of between $ 500 and $ 1,000 for moving expenses for jobs outside the local area. Nine employees took advantage of a $ 500 allowance for a job skills training course. (See Appendix III for full details.)

The redundancy package was greater than the amount provided under normal company policy, which was one week's pay per year of service, with an additional week for each year of service over forty years of age, up to a maximum of 52 weeks. In the case of Nobel, a minimum of $ 4,000 was paid to all employees regardless of age and service. Payments were made on a monthly basis over the following year. In order not to compromise company policy and set a precedent for higher payments in other closures, the company was very careful as to how the case for additional payments was presented. They were tied to the specific isolated location and the unique needs of the Nobel works. In other words, it was argued that higher payments were considered necessary here because there were very few alternative employment prospects, and there was also a high percentage of workers with relatively short service. Under normal conditions, these individuals would be heavily penalized by a package that "rewarded" age and service. Other closures, which involved workers in metropolitan areas, who would have fewer difficulties in finding other jobs, would not necessarily qualify for the same terms.

Union contracts linked redundancy to seniority, i. e. "last in, first out". Management was quite happy to adopt this system because of its apparently objective nature. It was considered to be a criterion that "workers relate to" and would avoid any problems concerning the choice of who was to be made redundant.

> The more acceptance you get of the selection process the better (manager).

In order to offset the effects of seniority and provide jobs for the younger members of the workforce, a voluntary early retirement package was offered. It was hoped that some of the older workers would take advantage of it, leaving their jobs open for others. The terms were the same as those being offered to redundant employees, except that early retirees qualified for their pension rights and were paid a retirement supplement to top off unemployment insurance (UIC) payments. Employees not otherwise eligible for retirement were thus offered a special retirement opportunity. Thirteen people took advantage of this. Management emphasized that it was a voluntary scheme and that no one was forced into taking it up. "The whole secret is giving them the option" (manager).

> [There was] less of a directive from the company – you weren't being forced, and people did have more choices. The more choices a person feels he has, the more he feels he is dealing with the crisis; rather than here's a crisis and we have no control (manager).

The Reasons

There were a number of reasons given for this particular approach to the closure and the package of benefits that was offered. One set of reasons revolved around the unique nature of Nobel which was situated in a small, isolated community. CIL was the major employer in the town. The only other large employer was also in danger of closing down, and with high unemployment in the area, it would have been very difficult for the affected employees to find work. Moreover, there was little chance of placing employees at other CIL plants in Ontario.

> The biggest worry was: what does this do to a factory like this; what does it do to a community like this. ... We were looking at ways of alleviating a pretty rotten situation in a small community (manager).

> Because Parry Sound is an isolated community, because we're the major employer, we tried to find as many things as possible to assist people in relocating and go beyond what we normally do (manager).

These factors, in the minds of divisional managers, necessitated generous redundancy terms. The $ 4,000 minimum was attributed to a basic premise that *everyone* would have difficulty in finding work regardless of age or service; and the fact that a large percentage of employees were relatively young and of short service (65 per cent of employees had less than ten years service, and more than half were under forty years of age).

The history of poor labour relations at the plant was another concern. There had been short illegal stoppages in 1974, 1975, 1976, and 1978, as well as legal strikes lasting 93 days in 1976 and 136 days in 1980. The union president exerted strong control over employees and was considered to have the capability to disrupt the shutdown. Management was concerned that the union had the power to engage in opposition to the closure, which they were anxious to avoid in case it spilled over into upcoming contract negotiations with the same union.

> [The previous history of bad labour relations] gave us a certain sensitivity about handling this because we could have had a very strong reaction to it. ... I don't think that that should be the only criteria that determines how you handle it, but it does play a role (manager).

> Labour relations at that plant are such that we were worried about negative repercussions. Would they [the union] go on strike? Would they walk out? Would there be sabotage and all these kinds of things? (manager).

The management – union relationship was particularly sensitive and important because of the decision to continue partial operations at the Nobel plant. Management was concerned that discontented employees might result in problems in the continuing part of the operation.

> [One should be] more careful if one is going to continue to be in the community. This means paying attention to the details so as not to cause problems, a need to maintain safety, morale, efficiency. Sabotage is a problem, especially in an explosives plant (manager).

> We wanted to continue to operate. We wanted to go out with a good relationship with our people so we could continue to have a satisfactory operation (manager).

CIL also considered its media profile to be important. It was anxious not to receive any bad publicity over the closure. A recent shutdown of a CIL subsidiary, as a result of its handling, had received considerable bad press which had damaged customer loyalty and government perceptions of the company.

Finally, managers took into account recent legislation and court settlements. Ontario legislation provided up to 26 weeks severance pay for employees with five or more years service, indicating that the government perceived compensation as a right rather than a privilege. The courts had been following this example, and the company did not want to become involved in any litigation over its redundancy payments.

Constraints and Facilitating Factors

One major help to CIL was the expertise gained in previous plant closures and layoffs. The Human Resource Group (HRG) had, as a result, developed a series of procedures to be used as a guideline for the handling of specific closures. In the case of Nobel, divisional management were fully supportive of the Human Resource Group's approach to closure.

> They [the divisional managers] were very sensitive – they wanted to do a good job. When you get that you get a minimum of problems (HRG manager).

The Human Resource Group is, however, a staff function, and its managers lack the formal authority to impose specific procedures on the divisions. Instead, they must try to persuade divisional managers to take their advice, which they do not always do.

> Nobel was a relatively good exercise. There have been others [closures] which have not been nearly as good. But that's the kind of variation we get. We'd like to be on record as saying we do them all that way [like Nobel] but that's not the case (HRG manager).
>
> There has sometimes been a struggle for control, here, [however] the division listened to us (HRG manager).

Corporate management was also amenable to the suggestions of how the closure should be managed. They made no major changes to the plan that was presented to them, and were willing to spend the necessary money. It has been suggested that the disastrous affair at the subsidiary, where little aid was provided for employees, had served to sensitize them to the issues involved. The plan still had to be "sold" on economic grounds, but the reasons presented by divisional management were considered sufficient to justify the cost of the redundancy package and the other support measures.

The company had time to plan the details of the closure. Following the decision to concentrate production at Beloeil rather than Nobel, a planning committee had been set up. For two months the members (including representatives from plant management, the Human Resource Group, and the Explosives Division) had examined the closure, its implications, and how best to manage it. When the official announcement of the closure was made, management had all the information available. This planning process had been carried out in secret. As time went on, however, the process was expanded to include more and more individuals, and the possibility of a leak increased. To safeguard against this situation, a contingency plan was prepared that would have brought the timing of everything forward, had a leak occurred.

> One of the biggest difficulties we have faced in trying to do a thorough job in managing these things is leaks. ... When the employee hears about the plant shutting down we want to make sure that at exactly the same time he hears about all the assistance efforts (manager).

Another problem related to secrecy emerged. It concerned the notice that had to be given to government departments in advance of the official announcement to employees. Representatives from the Ministry of Energy, Mines, and Resources; the Department of Economic and Regional Development; the Department of Industry, Trade, and Commerce; the Department of Regional Industrial Expansion; the Ministry of Employment and Immigration; and the Ministry of Labour had to be informed. Divisonal management delayed these announcements as long as possible to ensure that the closure was a carefully kept secret until employees were informed.

> We wanted to be able to explain to the employees ourselves the reasons why we were doing it and what we were going to do for them. We did not want the local politicians explaining it. Partly for selfish reasons because it's the only way you can get the story across in anything remotely like the truth, but more than anything else we wanted to be able to explain to the employees so they got it first hand (manager).

The Outcome

The outcome can be considered a success. There was little indication of bitterness, and ex-employees expressed satisfaction with the company's handling of the closure. Of the 176 people who were working at Nobel at the time of the closure, 53 were retained for the continuing part of the operation. Of the remaining 123, 58 were laid off, 13 took advantage of the early retirement program, 23 were transferred, 10 found new jobs outside the company, and 19 were retained for demolition of the plant. According to managers, productivity did not suffer and may actually have improved slightly after the closure. It was considered to be, partially, the result of the fear that the remaining operation might be phased out; but it also reflected how the closure was handled.

> It's amazing – if you manage the process well, sometimes productivity can go up (manager).

The cost of the program was $1.1 million (classified as an extraordinary item), and considered well worth it.

> We could not have bought such positive press for the money we spent (manager).

Management did not feel there is anything it would change.

> I think if people ask themselves if CIL treated them fairly, aside from the question of whether it was totally justified. I think the answer would probably be: compared with most other firms, yes, very well (manager).

Employees also seem to have been persuaded of the necessity of the closure.

> Everybody could see the writing on the wall. It was just a matter of time (manager).

The company continued to experience problems after the closure, particularly in 1985 and 1986, when the company incurred losses. The number of employees was reduced by one third between 1981 and 1987. The remaining operation at Nobel was closed in 1985 – employees were provided with twelve weeks' notice, and early retirement was offered to all employees over fifty years of age. The cost of this closure was estimated at $ 700,000. It was achieved without problems, which provides another indication that the original closure was managed successfully. Company performance improved recently and, in 1987, net income was 54 per cent higher than in 1983, return on investment 30 per cent higher, and return on equity 68 per cent higher.

Chapter 4: Whitefields

Whitefields is a large manufacturing multinational. Canadian operations have existed since 1917, and currently employ over 11,000 people with a turnover of more than $2 billion.

In 1982, employees with twenty-five or more years of service were offered a voluntary early retirement program (ERP) whereby they would receive 50 per cent of their salary for two years (or until they reached age sixty-five) following their retirement or resignation, effective by the end of February 1983. Eligible employees were notified by individual letter from the Vice-President (Personnel), followed by a seminar explaining the program and providing financial advice. Personnel managers checked that the letter had been received, worked out the details for individuals, and answered queries. External consultants provided counselling on the best way to protect income, and individuals were allowed personal investment counselling up to $2,500.

Expectations had been that out of the 1,288 individuals who were eligible for the program, about 200 would take advantage of it. In fact, double this number – 432 – actually did so. Of these only 16 were not retirees[1].

The reason for the early retirement program was due to the business recession in the 1980s. The formal operating plan for Canada in 1983, which was submitted to the company's headquarters, had had to be revised due to the recession. Lower revenue forecasts would not support existing numbers of personnel, and attrition, which had fallen as a result of the depressed economy, would not reduce numbers sufficiently. Therefore, the company decided to reduce the number of its personnel by offering some of them early retirement.

[1] Of the 1,288, 772 were eligible to retire (with thirty years service or age fifty-five). The remainder qualified with twenty-five years service, but were not eligible for early retirement. This latter group received the program's benefits, but their pension benefits were vested until they reached age fifty-five.

The Nature of the Early Retirement Program

The key characteristics of the program are, first, it was purely voluntary and, second, it involved retirements rather than layoffs. Both these characteristics were considered crucial in the light of the company's full employment practice, which protects employees against layoffs and promises them job security.

> Full employment in [the company] is a commitment on the part of management to maintain, through reasonable and practical efforts, steady employment for regular employees who are performing satisfactorily. Full employment is a practice rather than a policy. While it is not an absolute guarantee of employment, every ... chief executive has stated a strong commitment to the practice (company handbook).

Full employment is a practice rather than a policy, which means that its provisions are not an absolute right of employees, although the company undertakes to avoid actions that will involve layoffs. Nevertheless, the company is clearly committed to it, as a memo of December 1983 to all managers continued to emphasize.

> We've had a long tradition of full employment in [the company]. You and I must recognize the importance of this practice and do our very best to preserve it.

Enforced dismissals would clearly have violated the full employment practice. Even voluntary layoffs and voluntary dismissals would immediately cast doubt on the sincerity of the company in this matter.

This full employment practice is thus a significant constraint. It rules out anything other than voluntary methods of downsizing and puts pressure on managers to ensure that the process not only is voluntary, but is *perceived* as such by employees. The benefit of this approach is a stable internal environment that "eliminates the worry about jobs and financial security". In the opinion of Whitefields, it makes good business sense to:

> protect and maintain this investment in skilled experienced people, which is the most important ingredient in the company's formula for success (company handbook).

The constraining effects of this practice are not confined to limitations on the ways in which the company can reduce employee numbers. It must also ensure it has enough flexibility to obviate the need for rapid, large-scale job losses. In other words, Whitefields has to create a situation in which layoffs become unnecessary. One of the ways it does so is through retraining and transferring people from redundant positions to new jobs. Equally important is the conservative planning of human resource needs.

> Pursuing [the company's] full employment objective, therefore, requires a full-scale commitment, thorough planning and disciplined implementation. Because any hiring action has long-term implications for the company, hiring decisions are only made after detailed planning (company handbook).

And, because planning is never totally accurate, buffers are created with overtime, temporary employment, and subcontracted work. So, if business conditions deteriorate, costs can be recouped by reducing overtime or laying off temporary workers.

The full employment practice is thus a major commitment on the part of the company. It means careful, conservative planning to avoid hiring too many new employees. So, hiring during the next decade is expected to be significantly less than revenue growth. It also creates a challenge for managers responsible for downsizing programs. Voluntary programs are necessary if the full employment practice is to be respected, but it is difficult to predict the numbers of employees who will apply. In this case, the company was committed to accepting the number of applications, be they below or above expectations, and despite the short-term difficulties that may result.

> If no one had accepted it we wouldn't have fired anyone, we would have cut expenses and done other things first or carried the overload and not have been as profitable. We will make economic tradeoffs to protect full employment (manager).

The results of this approach to human resource management include a secure, productive, and flexible workforce and a highly profitable company. This profitability, in turn, provides the company with additional flexibility: Whitefields could, therefore, afford to offer a generous incentive and to absorb a certain amount of slack if numbers either exceeded, or failed to meet, expectations.

Another reason for the care with which human resources are protected in the company is the status of the personnel function. "Every manager is a personnel manager." The importance of human resources is emphasized in training, and numerous procedures exist to accommodate the company's obligation to its workforce. For example, retirees are contacted by their line managers every year, and special banquets are provided for all employees, including retirees, with twenty-five years service. Employees can ask to see any level of management if they feel they have not been fairly treated. Informal, confidential interviews are held between each employee and a manager at least one level above the individual's immediate manager. Surveys of employee attitudes are carried out on a voluntary, confidential basis with about 90 per cent participation. A suggestion plan offers $ 50 to $ 100,000 for successful proposals. One year, for example, 3,400 suggestions for cost savings were made, of which 672 were adopted. The awards totalled $ 500,000, while the company saved more than $ 3 million. Employees can voice, anonymously if they choose, complaints in a letter to the appropriate vice-president. The reply is returned within 10 days and copies of both are sent to the president. One year, there were 321 of them, of which 90 per cent were signed by the individuals concerned.

As a result of these practices, human relations and personnel management are highly valued functions in the company. Human resource managers expect line managers to follow their recommendations and procedures.

> We provide our managers with the information required to implement a program, and generally we expect that it's going to be implemented correctly (personnel manager).

The Outcome

The result of the early retirement program and, more precisely, the integrated system of personnel policies and practices, is a highly successful company with high productivity and sound employee relations. Profits between 1981 and 1985 almost doubled, and return on equity was consistently about 20 per cent. The early retirement program seems to have been a success from both the point of view of the company and the employees. People were, according to human resource managers, pleased that they took advantage of it; the voluntary nature did not compromise the full employment practice; and the standardized criteria (twenty-five years service) meant there was no stigma attached to those individuals who took early retirement. None of the 258 complaints sent to vice presidents following the program mentioned it. The program may even have reaffirmed the full employment policy, by allowing Whitefields employees to volunteer to leave, while those in other companies were being fired. The people who left received a generous package and, in most cases, a pension. From the company's point of view, the program was also a success: there were no complaints and the desired reduction was achieved. It provided prospects for revitalization by opening up promotional opportunities which, previously available through growth, had been curtailed through reduced hiring. Managers did not consider that the company had been adversely affected by the loss of key skills or experience.

Human resource managers did raise some concerns. They felt that people who just failed to qualify for the package expressed some resentment. Some managers felt that employees might alter their retirement plans in the future, in anticipation of another program being offered by the company. With only two such programs in more than eleven years, however, others felt this was not a major issue. Human resource managers pointed out that individual line managers did not always handle their employees with the same care and sensitivity. Finally, the increase in the number of retirees has presented a challenge for a company that places considerable importance in keeping in touch with them.

Conclusions

The key to understanding Whitefield's success lies in its global approach to employee relations. A small-scale voluntary early retirement program is a relatively pain-free way to downsize and comparatively easy to manage. However, in order for Whitefields to be in a position to manage its retrenchment in this way, it has had to devise an integrated approach to personnel issues. It includes cautious planning; the effective use of a variety of buffers, such as overtime, the use of temporary employees, and subcontracting; and a practice of full employment.

Human resource management in this company is a complex, long-term, and well-coordinated business, involving a great deal of money and time. An employee-oriented philosophy pervades the firm. In one way, this approach is constraining – decisions must be consistent since the company cannot afford to damage its credibility. In other ways, however, it results in a degree of flexibility which produces a highly profitable company.

Many organizations do not have human resource management so well integrated with their business planning systems. Whitefields shows how such integration can reduce the need for large-scale redundancies. As environments become more competitive, companies might be well advised to place more emphasis on the human resource element in their future strategies.

Summary: Managing the Interest Groups

The three organizations discussed in the preceding chapters all devoted a considerable amount of effort to the political side of retrenchment. They all considered that the key to successful cutbacks – and turnaround – was to ensure that employees and other stakeholders were not alienated by the retrenchment program. These organizations were able to pursue this goal relatively unhampered by short-term economic constraints. While the various cutbacks were obviously undertaken in response to economic difficulties, all three companies were large enough and rich enough to subsidize the costs of the retrenchment program. This section examines these issues in more detail.

ICI management had identified a number of interest groups which it considered to have the potential to disrupt the closure and otherwise interfere with the company's plans. Of primary concern was union resistance which, if it occurred, could easily escalate to other factories and damage the division as a whole. Resistance would also jeopardize the complicated rundown schedule which had been devised to allow the uninterrupted transfer of production to other sites. ICI also had no wish to antagonize the unions with the prospect of other closures in the near future. This desire to avoid union resistance obviously meant that employees' needs were an important factor, which managers took into account during the closure. Cost constraints, however, were less pressing. The company had been very profitable in the 1970s (Pettigrew, 1985). The works manager admitted that he had had considerable latitude in how he carried the closure out and had been "very liberal with the company's money". ICI also had considerable time to plan and prepare for the closure since, as early as 1971, the works manager knew that the works would be closed eventually. In summary, divisional managers were clearly committed to a smooth closure, and possessed both the funds and time necessary to enable them to achieve it.

So, how was this money and time spent? The company started early in preparing for a successful closure. It commenced the rundown process, in effect, in 1971, when a new works manager was appointed to change the authoritarian culture and create a climate far more favourable to the management of cutbacks. ICI also issued a statement in 1975, shortly before the closure was announced, saying that enforced dismissals would occur "only as a last resort". In order to achieve the desired reduction of 40 per cent of personnel, voluntary severance was used. Remaining numbers were accommodated by attrition and redeployment. The company provided outplacement support to these employees to help them find new jobs.

The major potential threat to the company's plan was the group of senior shop stewards which represented the various blue-collar unions. If resistance to the closure had occurred, it would, almost inevitably, been orchestrated and organized by this group. As a result, a committee was set up, consisting of managers and senior stewards, to make recommendations on the rundown. In this way, the stewards were able to become involved in, and have a positive impact on, the rundown process.

As a result of these actions, the closure proceeded according to the timetable, accepted by the majority of shop stewards and union officials, who considered ICI one of the better employers in this respect. No industrial action was taken, all discussions were handled at the local level, and there were no grievances. Productivity remained stable, absenteeism and customer complaints fell. Employees had no criticism of how the company had handled the closure and were grateful for the various benefits that had been provided.

CIL was also concerned about the power of its union. Managers were anxious to avoid sabotage, nor did they want to alienate the union when contract negotiations were coming up. The morale of continuing employees was considered to be an important factor, since part of the operation would continue to operate, at least in the short term. As with ICI, there was a prospect of further cuts and, in fact, the remaining operation was subsequently closed in 1985. Finally, the company wanted to avoid bad publicity. An earlier closure, handled by a subsidiary, had attracted considerable criticism from the press which, it was felt, had damaged CIL's reputation in the eyes of its employees, its customers, and the public. The cost of the program did not present any major problems. Divisional management was committed to providing a package which would protect their employees and had secured approval from the senior executive level for the amount of money (close to $ 1 million) which it would cost. Managers also had several months in which they were able to prepare plans and procedures for the rundown process.

CIL used some of the time it had to provide employees with five months advance notice of the closure. They provided severance pay to all employees, based on the specific needs of the Nobel location. Layoffs were determined by seniority, according to the collective agreement. The company also offered an early retirement package to free up some jobs for younger employees. Placement committees, with employee and management representation, were established to deal with outplacement needs. Job search counselling and expenses were provided, relocation expenses paid, and time off to attend interviews made available without loss of pay.

As a result of these measures, the partial closure was caried out without sabotage or union resistance. Productivity rose and the scene was set for the successful closure of the remaining part of the operation.

The main factor guiding *Whitefields* was its full employment practice which effectively protected employees against enforced layoffs, and which the company was unwilling to compromise. The result was an early retirement program. Management was willing to bear the cost of the program – two years' pay over the following four years – and the uncertainty involved. Had insufficient numbers applied, the company was willing to carry the additional overhead rather than invoke more drastic measures.

While both ICI and CIL had some time in which to prepare for retrenchment – ranging from a few months to a few years –, Whitefield's approach was embodied in an even more long-term perspective. Human resources are fully integrated into business and business planning in a way that helps the company to avoid the dismissal of full-time employees. The existence of this integrated human resource strategy meant that the downsizing exercise could be carried out in a purely voluntary manner, and in such a way that it was not even viewed by employees as a form of layoff.

I.2 Balancing Economic and Political Pressures

Chapter 5: Andersons

Andersons is a non-British based multinational, which, in 1980, closed a factory known here as Newlands, situated in the west of Scotland. The factory had been operating in the general areas of mechanical engineering since 1949, employing about 1,500 people.

Andersons experienced more dramatic economic problems then CIL, ICI, or Whitefields. In September 1978, following a worldwide loss of $ 145 million for the nine months ending 31 July and appointment of a new president, U.K. management announced that a study was to be conducted into the European manufacture of product A, which was produced at Newlands and St. Bertin, France. The study was to examine the most efficient manufacturing arrangements for product A, given that the company had excess manufacturing capacity at its two European plants; and to ascertain the best utilization of any capacity which was released.

The recommendations were presented in November 1978, a month earlier than anticipated. They proposed the complete transfer of product A to St. Bertin, in order to save $ 10 million on annual overheads. It was also suggested that a second product (product B) should be transferred from St. Bertin to Newlands which, at a cost of $ 2 million, would provide work for 500 people. The latter recommendations was, according to the company, in recognition of its social obligation to its workforce and the area.

These recommendations were presented to employees and union officials, who responded quickly. Local stewards formed a Joint Union Coordinating Committee (JUCC) which consisted of nine representatives of both manual and staff unions[1]. Members of a local university were commissioned to study the commercial basis of Anderson's deci-

[1] The main unions were the Amalgamated Union of Engineering Workers (AUEW), the Technical, Administrative, and Supervisory Section of the AUEW (TASS) and the Association of Professional, Executive, Chemical, and Computer Staff (APEX).

sion. A second study was conducted into the social implications of the decision. The coordinating committee lobbied politicians and other unions. They organized a demonstration in London, and arranged a visit to the French factory to see if they could learn anything there.

In January 1979, the unions presented their case to the company. They argued that product A should continue to be manufactured at Newlands and product B in France. They also pointed, on the basis of the second study, to the severe effect the company's decision would have on the local economy. A series of meetings evolved concerning the studies during which managers tried to explain their position. They were, however, unable to "prove" their arguments to the satisfaction of union officials because the company would not allow the release of the figures on which the recommendations had been based. As a result, the discussions led to a stalemate and eventually petered out.

In July 1979, the company reopened the study and extended the deadline for the final decision. This was followed by another series of meetings between the president, the Scottish Trades Union Congress, the unions, the local stewards, and the district council, and also between the U.K. managing director, local members of Parliament, the Under-Secretary of State for Scottish Industry, and the Secretary of State for Industry. These meetings revolved around the future of the factory and the possibilities of saving jobs. Economic problems continued to plague the company and, in November 1979, following the collapse of the market for product B, it was announced that there would be a complete closure of Newlands with the loss of 1,500 jobs in February 1980.

In the meantime, consultants had been brought in to work out new payment and production systems in anticipation of the arrival of product B. These consultants had been liaising with both managers and employees, as a result of which an idea had emerged for bringing alternative work into the factory. An international search had been conducted by the company to try and find a buyer for the complete factory, which the company was prepared to sell for a nominal sum. While it proved unsuccessful, a local search had also been established, involving both managers and employees. It uncovered a small demand for the employees' engineering skills. As a result, Andersons helped to set up a new company – Merryvale Ltd – by providing financial resources and managerial expertise. Merryvale was to operate on part of the original site and employ some of the workers.

In February 1980, Andersons withdrew from the Newlands site, leaving Merryvale Ltd, which employed about 200 people from Newlands. Andersons was responsible for the project, but wished to hold no more than a 20 per cent share of the company in the long term.

The Process

Managers at Andersons were faced with a highly volatile situation. They wanted to close a factory in an area where alternative jobs were hard to find since the unemployment rate was 50 per cent higher than the national average. They were concerned that the unions might stage an occupation of the factory and prevent the closure. The area was famous for a number of closures that had occurred in the 1970s and which had provoked factory occupations. What strengthened this threat was the previous militancy of the workforce. For example, a strike and lockout had occurred in 1977, which had resulted in 18 per cent of hours being lost through industrial action. Moreover, following the announcement of the possible transfer of production to France, the local stewards had been quick to organize. They had formed a joint commmittee and called in union officials. Management felt, as a result, that there was a strong possibility of resistance from the employees since both the motivation – the lack of alternative jobs – and the means – a strong militant union – existed.

> We were never confident that it was going to go our way. We were never certain whether or not it was going to turn into an occupation; it was always on the cards (U.K. director).

Management was anxious to avoid both a strike and an occupation at Newlands. Local stewards had obtained pledges of support from other British factories. If they took industrial action, it could easily escalate into a national strike, jeopardizing the entire U.K. operation and creating problems for the smooth transfer of production to France. U.K. managers were also anxious to prove to their corporate heads in North America that they could manage a closure effectively. The U.K. division had long had a reputation for difficulties with intransigent unions – their North American counterparts had had far fewer problems and, as a result, were earning considerably more favour from the corporate level.

Unlike ICI or even CIL, U.K. management had been able to do little to prepare for the news of the feasibility study and prospective job losses. U.K. managers had learned of the company's decision only two or three weeks before the official announcement was to be made. They were, then, unable to do anything to offset the previously tense relations between management and the unions before job losses became a very real possibility. They were faced with a situation in which they had to counteract the bad news, *after* it had been transmitted, in order to reduce the likelihood of resistance. The tactic that was adopted was the promotion of the idea that, if the unions cooperated, there was a chance of saving at least some of the jobs.

> Our aim was to perpetually convince people that war would have a bad effect and they would lose out; that peace gave them hope and a chance (U.K. director).
>
> People perpetually had hope that something would come out of it that would leave them with jobs (U.K. director).

First, there was the (faint) possibility of retaining product A, or at least having product B transferred to the Scottish factory. As those prospects dimmed, the international and local work searches provided another chance to salvage some jobs. Finally, there was Merryvale Ltd, which employed about 200 individuals. All these measures, which rested on the cooperation of the employees, represented the opportunity to protect some jobs, while discouraging industrial action.

> The one thing we couldn't afford was bad publicity because if you're trying to entice a company in and the company sees there's trouble, they're not going to come (member of JUCC).

A second part of the company's strategy was the provision of redundancy payments which were two to three times the legal minimum. The academics felt they proved to be too powerful an inducement for the old, long-serving workforce. (Over 55 per cent were aged forty-five years or more. More than 25 per cent of hourly paid and 48 per cent of staff had over twenty years service.) A large proportion of the workforce received substantial compensation, which undoubtedly tempted them to accept the closure.

> We might have gone on strike but it wouldn't have done any good – we might have lost out on redundancy pay (employee).

A third element of the strategy was consultation. First, a study was produced on the location of production, which management was apparently willing to discuss before reaching a final decision. One reason for this was, according to management, to see if the union could come up with viable suggestions for preventing redundancies. More importantly, however, it was to avoid the mistake of making a procedural error:

> to make sure that in no way could we be criticized for not having given the trade unions every opportunity to be consulted (U.K. director).

In reality, however, the contribution of the unions to the decision-making process was limited. Management did not allow the unions to participate in the feasibility study and was not willing to release confidential figures. Nevertheless, the unions and stewards did take up the consultative path. They prepared their own report, having accepted, to a great extent, the economic rationale provided by the company. Unions and stewards thought that the only way to save the factory was to demonstrate that Newlands was an economically viable plant. Unfortunately, they did not have access to the crucial figures that were necessary to prove their case.

> We were using a method of argument which in the end we could never win. For every set of statistics we attacked, the company would come back and produce new ones (academic involved in the union report, in published article, 1981).

This strategy was highly successful for management because, by becoming involved in the consultative process, opposition groups were directed away from more confrontational forms of action.

> The focussing of our work on the accounts may have meant that other avenues were not explored (academic in published article, 1981).

The dialogue which arose from the studies helped to defuse the issue. Although union officials believed at the time that this strategy was the only way to save the factory, they may, by "buying into" management's arguments, have achieved the opposite.

> It is possible that the contribution we made helped to reinforce, quite inadvertently, a strategy which, in the end, has produced the closure of that factory (academic in published article, 1981).

Another aim of the consultation was to reduce the possibility of resistance by convincing employees and unionists of the need to relocate production in France. Managers met with only limited success.

Their argument was that the redundancies and eventual closure were necessary to save money and that, given market conditions, dual sourcing was not justified. The union report, however, saw the closure of Newlands as less of an economic response, than a political strategy aimed at placating external stakeholders, which were unhappy with the results of previous mismanagement.

> The inclusion of [Newlands] in the cost-saving action programme is a cosmetic exercise designed to placate the financial institutions and reassure the investors who have seen their share values drop by two-thirds in less than two years ... This crisis is not centrally one of markets or of excess capacity, although these problems do exist. The reason for the precipitate search for a means to actually close a plant lies in previous bad management decisions ... and pressure from international financial institutions (union report).

Many employees also believed that Newlands had been selected for closure specifically because of its previous history of militant unions. Management did, however, have some success in convincing employees of the precarious position of the company as a whole, and that resistance at Newlands could have adverse complications for the other U.K. factories.

> The things had to be done or the company itself would collapse. Nobody wants the company to collapse, because there are a lot of people employed there (member of JUCC).

The Outcome

Management succeeded in closing Newlands without industrial action: no mean achievement given the volatility of the situation. In addition, it won praise and respect for the handling of the closure and for saving some jobs.

> I believe that there was some sort of social conscience, if you can believe that in a multinational company (steward).
>
> They accepted their social responsibility – they had a conscience (local council official).
>
> I think they did try not to leave the place with a hostile relationship (union official).

> When [Andersons] decided to close its plant at [Newlands] in Scotland it did not just abandon its workforce. Instead it got together with them and tried to find a new use for the factory, so that [Andersons] would not leave its workers without jobs in an area of already high unemployment [trade journal).

These sentiments did not, however, extend to many of the people who had lost their jobs as a result of the closure, amongst whom there was considerable bitterness. Ex-employees felt that people had been "sold short"; that the company "should have paid more money"; and that they were "unfair" and "ruthless'.

Andersons also received criticism for not consulting in good faith. One problem concerned the early report of the feasibility study. Union officials felt that "for them to do a feasibility study in such a short time was impossible". They were convinced it was a cosmetic exercise designed to justify a decision that had already been taken. This view was strengthened by the fact that the unions had not been allowed to participate, and that key figures had not been released.

> Management, in their typical style, was prepared to listen ... but, at the end of the day, they were still intending to carry on with their proposals (steward).

Nevertheless, Andersons provides an example of how a difficult situation, in terms of a very real threat of resistance, can be managed. Andersons' goal of avoiding conflict was made more difficult by the strength of the unions and the history of confrontation, and the short time lag between U.K. management learning of the planned feasibility study and its announcement to employees. Andersons' strategy avoided overt confrontation and helped to produce more favourable perceptions of the company among employee and union groups.

In terms of the health of the organization as a whole, Andersons has continued to experience major problems that prompted both the rescheduling of the company's debt and a company-wide reorganization. Massive losses were incurred in 1980, 1981, 1982, 1983, and 1984. A series of layoffs and closures were conducted into the 1980s, and by 1984, there were 40 per cent fewer people working for Andersons than in 1979. This trend continued and 1988 figures show a company that has over 70 per cent fewer employees than a decade earlier. In 1985, the company managed to post a slim profit, for the first time since 1979. Losses were, once again, the story in 1987, although a small profit was posted in 1988.

Chapter 6: Atomic Energy of Canada Ltd

Atomic Energy of Canada Ltd (AECL) is a crown corporation (state-owned enterprise) charged with developing, "for national benefit, the peaceful uses of nuclear technology". It was established in 1952 and reports to Parliament through the Minister of Energy, Mines, and Resources. AECL employs 7,000 individuals who are responsible for designing and marketing nuclear power stations and technology, engaging in research, providing nuclear engineering skills, manufacturing specialized industrial and medical equipment, and operating the heavy water production plants.

The corporate office is in Ottawa; the corporation is divided into three operating groups; research and development; commercial products; and Candu Operations. The latter, with which this chapter is concerned, is based at Mississauga, Ontario and is involved in the manufacture of Candu nuclear power stations. In 1982, about 2,500 people were employed there.

The 1970s had been productive for AECL. The mid-1970s brought contracts from Korea and Argentina as well as domestic sources, resulting in more than a dozen projects. At the end of the 1970s, hiring continued to be a major preoccupation and, as late as 1981, 1981/82 graduates were still being hired. By December of that year, however, the situation changed dramatically. Most of the reactor projects were coming to an end in 1982, and no replacement orders had been forthcoming due to a worldwide drop in demand. When the tender for a Mexican project fell through, it became clear Candu Operations could no longer sustain a workforce of 2,500.

As a result, a hiring freeze was imposed. In August of 1982, the need for cost reduction measures was announced, and exploratory talks with employee and union groups (the Society of Professional Engineers and Associates – SPEA, and the Public Service Alliance of Canada – PSAC) commenced. On November 8th, the company announced 600 layoffs in Candu operations, mainly in the Mississauga plant, as part of a plan to reduce work levels and budgets by 25 per cent.

The Layoff Process

Individuals were selected for redundancy according to seniority, with allowances made for certain key skills. Individuals received sixteen weeks or more advance notice; outplacement aid and severance pay were provided; consultation took place through various committee structures including a Joint Planning Committee (JPC) and Joint Manpower Adjustment Committees (JMACs). The JPC's terms of reference concerned the whole plant and was required by law. In addition, the company set up JMACs to deal with the specific needs of four employee groups; the two unions and two nonunionized groups – administrative and technical staff (see Appendix IV).

The layoffs were to be accomplished in two phases: the bulk in February and March 1983, the remainder in September 1983. A Manpower Steering Committee (MSC) was established in September 1982 to address the policy issues associated with the downsizing, and to evaluate critical skills. It was chaired by the Vice-President (Engineering) and consisted of other vice-presidents who established a subcommittee of middle managers to identify those individuals to be laid off. The MSC was unable to produce 600 names, so the layoffs were broken down into the two phases: the first during February and March 1983, when the 510 individuals which had been identified would leave; the remainder were to leave later that year.

The remainder of this section examines the components of the layoff process in more detail.

Advance Notice

Advance notice was tied in with AECL's obligation, under the Canada Labour Code, to provide sixteen weeks notice of group layoffs. Strictly speaking, the individual employee was entitled to only two weeks notice. AECL felt, however, that the uncertainty which would result from the workforce knowing that one quarter of them would lose their jobs, but not knowing exactly who would be affected, would be seriously disruptive. Consequently, the corporation decided to issue group and individual notices at the same time.

> If you had let it be known beforehand that you were laying off one quarter of the company, then you would have had the whole company

> worried, rather than the specific quarter, and I think that would have had a tremendous effect on production (manager).

Opinion in the corporation was divided concerning the benefits of advance notice. Some, particularly in line management positions, felt that production suffered during the period leading up to the actual layoffs.

> As it turned out we gave three, nearly four, months notice and it took strong, determined managers to keep production up (manager).

Others felt, however, that the alternative would have had a worse effect, and that, if production fell, it was due more to the committees and seminars that employees were attending during working hours, rather than anxiety over impending job loss. Critics also asserted that, because of the long time between notification and termination, employees failed to accept the fact that they had been made redundant, or get on with the task of looking for a new job. They were of the opinion that a more immediate break with the company would have been better, perhaps with some outplacement facilities provided off-site.

> The law is based on the misapprehension that keeping people working is to their advantage. I think what's to their advantage is to give them some space, some leadership on how to find a job (executive).

Representatives of the unions and members of the Human Resource Division (HRD), however, believed that:

> While there are some negative aspects [of advance notice]; from a psychological view, it helps if the employee is still employed when he looks for a new job ... It helps him to sell himself to his new employer (union representative).
>
> Philosophically, I think the maximum notice is a good thing. It allows people to adjust and find other jobs (HRD manager).
>
> Advance notice is necessary to give people the opportunity to look for new work while they are still employed. It helps mentally (employee).

With hindsight, the company decided that any disadvantages connected with the advance notice were compensated for by the help it provided employees.

> AECL recognizes some of the disadvantages known to be associated with lengthy periods of notice, nevertheless the company felt that

> its redundant employees deserved the benefit of considerable notice particularly in the light of the difficult job market they would face (Report on the Company Assistance Program).

Selective Dismissals

The basis of the selection process was seniority, but with allowances made for people who possessed skills that AECL considered critical to its future. The company believed that, to protect its future viability in a difficult environment, certain skills had to be retained.

> Any organization like this, that wants to stay alive has to think into the future and not just the present and not simply chop off individuals willy nilly. They have to look at what survival in the 1980s is going to mean (manager).

So, in some cases, seniority was circumvented to protect these skills.

> Had we laid off in strict seniority in unionized and non-unionized sectors the company would collapse. We just [wouldn't be able to] cope with the [skilled] people we would lose (manager).

Some line managers felt the company did not go far enough in selecting the people it wished to retain.

> There is no doubt that we would have a somewhat better workforce had we been able to get away from seniority and [had] some ability to pick and choose more. Seniority did do damage to us, did lose us of our younger fresher blood, more promising people. It did keep in the organization individuals who were not contributing that effectively (manager).

Other managers felt that adhering strictly to seniority would have been a better mechanism, since it helped people:

> view the thing in a rational fashion so they can accept the choices that were made (manager).

The problem at AECL was that, once the principle of seniority was disbanded, some individuals, at least, were selected for dismissal on political or personal grounds, as some managers have admitted.

> [The MSC] was highly political. If the group knew the person being discussed, the decision was based on what they thought of them (manager).

Other managers argued that seniority was side-stepped only to remove marginal performers.

> There are some cases of some well-established non-performers who are no longer with us. There was much grumbling but maybe a little respect too (manager).
>
> One of my intentions was to use this as an opportunity to weed out dead wood ... When you have to retrench, you really have to identify the non-performers, regardless of what the rules are (manager).

Employees and some managers felt, however, that redundancies and dismissals for performance reasons should be kept separate; that redundant employees should not in any way have the stigma of poor performance attached to them.

> Our belief is that layoff is not the same as firing (union representative).

They felt that the very existence of "dead wood" showed that the company had not been effective in supervising performance before the layoffs, probably as a result of the massive expansion in the 1970s. They thought the retrenchment program should not have been an excuse to rectify poor managerial decisions.

Stepping out of line with seniority resulted in a number of grievances. There were 57 grievances concerning SPEA (The Engineers' Union), of which 19 resulted in reinstatement. The 14 grievances involving Public Service Alliance members were resolved through the grievance procedure. There were charges that the non-unionized groups, without the protection of a contract, suffered more from the violation of seniority.

> There has been some concern that some of the people who have been terminated in non-bargaining units are perhaps less representative of seniority. There has been a tendency to get rid of the higher priced technical people and replace them with junior professionals (employee).

Managers disputed this accusation.

> We went through a major exercise [in MSC] before the layoffs trying to come up with some principles about selections for layoff. It was a major battle in management whether we should respect seniority for non-unionized people. Our general philosophy is that we treat non-union staff as equals [vis-à-vis unionized employees] in terms of all conditions and requirements, so we won the fight to have seniority considered as the major term (manager).

> We were walking a fine line because we had to convince senior management that where there was an obvious case of a mistake, even though they are non-union and even though they can't take it to arbitration, if this process is going to work, you are going to have to give in on some of those people (manager).

Managers argued that they took equal care with both union and non-union groups. Administrative employees brought 26 grievances, which resulted in 3 reinstatements. Technical employees were involved in similar numbers. Grievance procedures were specially introduced for the benefit of these two nonunionized groups which, previously, had not had access to them. Employees were satisfied with the fact that such procedures had been introduced, but they felt they had had a limited impact.

> The people in the grievance committee worked hard. They didn't uphold many of the grievances but they were fair (union representative).

Voluntary Dismissals

Some of the complaints regarding the selective nature of the dismissals might have been avoided, if a voluntary program had been offered prior to the selective terminations. Such a scheme was made available, but only eight months afterwards, at the same rates as the severance package. The target was principally retirees, but a number of others came forward which resulted in more than eighty people taking advantage of the offer.

The company had been reluctant to adopt a program of voluntary terminations, believing that the required numbers would not have been forthcoming without a prohibitive financial commitment.

> A voluntary scheme would not have given us those [required] numbers. If you make a package rich enough you would get the number that you want. Unfortunately we didn't feel, financially, that that was appropriate. We did have a voluntary package that came later, which was not a rich package (manager).

It has been argued that the president only approved the voluntary package when it was made clear that there would be a positive result on the overall workforce reduction program without any additional expense. The company was also reluctant to institute a voluntary program for fear of losing control over who left. It did not want the good people to leave while the marginal performers stayed.

Members of the Human Resource Division, employees, and union representatives did not share this view. They felt that, even without an additional incentive, some people would have taken advantage of a voluntary program had it been offered beforehand. Thus, it would have had two important benefits: jobs would have been freed; and the company would have been seen to be doing its utmost to accommodate the needs of the employees. They also disputed that a voluntary program would have caused a mass exodus of the best employees.

> [People have] certain loyalties and commitments to the company. These factors keep the people here regardless of the job market (union representative).

Consultation

Another feature of the layoffs was the use of consultation committees: A Joint Planning Committee (JPC) and four Joint Manpower Adjustment Committees (JMACs). AECL was one of the first employers to conduct a layoff under the new provisions of the Canada Labour Code for group termination of employment (Part III, Division V.2), which required a JPC to be set up. The new legislation thus not only required consultation, but also prescribed its structure, with representation of union and of non-union groups on the JPC. The company felt, however, that the four employee groups that it had identified had different interests and would overburden the JPC, and so it established a JMAC for each of the four groups. They worked on a similar basis to the JPC with employee/union representation and an independent chairman; the difference being that each JMAC dealt solely with the issues of an individual group (see Appendix IV for terms of reference).

> Items peculiar to each group, e. g. employee grievances, [would] be discussed in this forum. The JPC could then be left to address global issues, particularly those advanced subsequent to JMAC discussion (Report on the Company Assistance Program).

These committees met weekly or every two weeks from November to June, and subcommittees were struck to deal with outplacement and grievances. The former were responsible for examining ways of helping ex-employees look for new jobs. The latter were used to resolve the grievances which arose from alleged transgressions of seniority by the company. Grievance procedures already existed for the unionized groups and were established for the non-union groups.

Employees became disenchanted with the JPC, saying that the company was unwilling to discuss the details of the redundancy package. It was "bolting the stable door after the horse had gone because the company had already made its decisions".

> JPC was a railroad job. Management had no intention of listening. They had to go through the motions because it was required by law (JPC member).

Managers agreed with this interpretation.

> We were not prepared to negotiate the plan we had put together [because] the plan was a good one (manager).
>
> To some extent we were not prepared to consult; we had decided what we were going to do and how we were going to do it (manager).

They argued that they had found it difficult enough to deal with the complexity of the retrenchment, without broadening the decision-making process further.

> This was a very complex issue. We hardly understood it ourselves, let alone knew how to go about doing it. I think the idea of other inputs that we couldn't deal with [worried us because it] would only cause the whole process to become unmanageable (manager).
>
> We were having a hell of a time making sense of all this and it was very hard to absorb any other inputs, especially if it could reverse things we had already got launched on (manager).

AECL's view was that while some form of consultation and communication was required, the Joint Planning Committee presented the company with an untenable process. Management felt that the primary concerns of the employees should have been outplacement and grievances. These issues are where employees:

> focussed most of their interest and activity, and that's where it should have been right from the start ... It wasn't in the interests of the employees to try to reverse the decision or try to get more compensation. The company has made these decisions and they are irrevocable, so let's try and get on with the business of finding jobs (manager).

The JPC was, therefore, not the type of committee that managers wanted.

> Would we have created a JPC without the requirement of the legislation? No, because it didn't seem appropriate ... our attention would have been on an alternate structure, more on JMAC lines ... In terms of the benefits provided for employees, we would have done that (manager).

While managers were reluctant to discuss alternative ways in which the downsizing could be accomplished, employees felt that it was important to discuss ways of saving jobs or, at least, improving the conditions of the reduction program. At least, part of the impetus for the eventual adoption of a voluntary early retirement package came from employees. So, from the employees' viewpoint, the exploration of alternative ways of saving jobs was not contrary to their interests. Employees criticized managers for not using the JPC in good faith.

> Sometimes I thought they [the company] told us what we wanted to hear (employee).
>
> Our opinion is that the company appreciated us when we agreed with them, but [did not find it] quite so digestible when we disagreed (JMAC member).

The inability of the JPC to implement alternatives to enforced dismissals further confirmed opinions that management was not sincere. The voluntary package was offered only after the majority of layoffs; while other alternatives, including worksharing involving a temporary 10 per cent reduction in working hours, leave without pay, and active outplacement to other sites, were rejected. JPC members felt that the company had simply refused to consider any of these alternatives seriously.

> We presented [our] alternatives, and they were completely rejected out of hand (JPC member).

The Joint Manpower Adjustment Committees, on the other hand, met with approval from employee representatives, who considered them more of a "two-way dialogue" than the JPC. The outplacement and grievance subcommittees were considered particularly effective.

> It was a two-way process, and it was a working committee: we didn't just sit in meetings and make lofty decisions (union representative).

Non-unionized groups were particularly appreciative of the JMACs.

> Without the JMACs there was no way for people not in bargaining units to be terminated and have their grievances reviewed in a fairly unbiased recommendation (JMAC member).

The non-unionized JMACs have been continued as communication committees to improve the general level of communication in the company.

> I think that general management and employee relations could be improved with much more vigorous communications, discussions and greater openness and disclosure of what happens at executive and senior management levels (manager).

Outplacement

The people who lost their jobs had access to outplacement aid, which involved a number of measures. A general information session was held following the cutback announcement to address such issues as: severance and benefit entitlements; the aid that would be provided; consultation; and specific questions from employees. External consultants conducted a two-day seminar on job searching techniques. After-hours instruction on interviewing techniques and financial counselling was set up. The Human Resource Division made its expertise available to employees in a number of ways: resumé preparation, reference letters, "ad tracking", exploratory letters to potential employers, advertising of available skills, posting of internal job opportunities, personal counselling, and staffing of an outplacement centre where jobs were posted. A job fair was arranged in which potential employers were invited to the site.

The company provided each redundant employee with severance pay, including a supplement to the company's normal arrangements. It worked out to 2 weeks pay for the first, and 1 week's pay for each additional year of service up to a maximum of 30 weeks pay (standard policy) plus an additional one half day for each full month of service while under age 45 (8 days minimum, 25 days maximum), and 1 day for each full month of service while over age 45 (8 days minimum, 50 days maximum). Employees received paid time away from work to attend interviews and seminars. If employees resigned before their layoff date, they did not necessarily lose their severance pay.

This outplacement aid was a resounding success. AECL did a "very good job", according to Engineering Union and others.

> I really don't know what more they could have done (union representative).

> It was handsomely done, especially when you compare it with what just about everybody else is doing (manager).

The success of outplacement depends on the state of the economy and, at that time, it was a bad time to be looking for a job. Nevertheless, people were placed. Of 26 terminated members of the Public Service Alliance, 8 had been placed by June 1st, 1983. Of 102 terminated engineers, 56 had been placed by the same date.

> Aside from the slack job market, there were no serious problems encountered by the [outplacement] committee. Certainly, outplacement aids and resources were readily available and there was no lack of effort on the part of the JMAC itself or by the Human Resources staff of AECL (Report of SPEA JMAC).

Some people failed to make use of the available facilities. For example, for the seminar on interview techniques, 100 people were contacted, 40 expressed interest, 13 registered, but only 4 actually attended (source: Newsheet of Administrative Joint Manpower Adjustment Committee). These problems have been attributed to the individuals concerned, who were seen by some managers to be "their own worst enemies". One solution that was suggested was to hold such seminars during worktime as, for example, the initial seminar at which 98 per cent attendance was recorded, and the job fair which 77 per cent of terminated employees attended.

The Lack of Planning

The downsizing announcement came very much as a shock to employees, following so closely on the busy years of the 1970s.

> The thing about the economy came upon us very suddenly. We had had, for so many years, nuclear projects of a long time. We had been accustomed to looking ahead and seeing this horrendous mountain of work. Suddenly here was this huge number of projects that we had been working on beginning to dry up on us (manager).

The problems of the 1970s had been finding sufficiently qualified individuals to staff projects, and managing growth. As a result, AECL was not used to thinking about contraction. As one manager put it: "generals tend to fight their last campaigns". Others have pointed out, however, that long-term strategic and human resource planning were not among the company's strengths.

> I don't think senior management was ready to face up to the prospect of layoffs at that time and, even though the numbers show that things were going definitely wrong and we would have to do something, senior management did not want to think about it (manager).

It was this short-sightedness that led to the abrupt turnaround in the hiring situation. Graduates, only hired in 1981/2, lost their jobs in 1983. They were understandably upset at losing their jobs so quickly.

> We, the 1982 Graduate Engineers and Scientists, are very disappointed with the outcome of the recent terminations. Upon discussion between the graduates, the common view was shared that the terms of our employment have not been fulfilled ... Had we not been attracted to AECL's [training program], many of the graduates would have accepted the promises of challenging careers elsewhere (memorandum from the 1982 Graduate Engineers and Scientists, November 1982).
>
> The Society strongly objected to the continued hiring of new graduates, especially when they were not being told of declining business conditions (SPEA Report).

The Reasons

One of the major reasons for the choice of AECL's retrenchment strategy concerns its status as a crown corporation. The company was driven by a desire to be business oriented and, at the same time, maintain a low profile, so as not to offend political sensitivities.

> As a crown corporation we do have political visibility. [It] was an incentive to be very cautious about this entire process, to plan it carefully so it could stand up to close scrutiny – political and public ... There's no question, there was political sensitivity (manager).

Political sensitivity meant, in the eyes of AECL managers, that the company should be seen to be acting responsibly and avoid a bad image – or even too good an image, which could result in accusations of wasting taxpayers' money.

> One of the strongest constraints in our layoff was that we did not wish to be featured on the CBC, in the Globe & Mail, or anywhere else. We succeeded in that, perhaps by being too conservative (manager).

> We wanted to avoid any excessive media attention, and if we did attract media attention, we wanted to be seen to be doing the right thing ... We are very defensive regarding the media. I'm not sure that's the right strategy but it's the one we're using right now and it would take a large concentrated effort to do otherwise (manager).

The result was a odd mixture of social responsibility and the bottom line.

> [We are trying to be] fair to people without exposing the company to a huge expense that's not necessary, that's not justified. We're not trying to be the best employer in the world, we're not trying to be the worst – we're trying to be a good employer (executive).

It was this business philosophy that resulted in the reluctance to adopt a voluntary program. Another reason stemmed form the status of human resources inside the company. It was the opinion of many that the Human Resource Division (HRD) had limited power in this engineers-dominated company.

> We on the union side felt that the HRD people were just frontmen. They weren't making decisions, they were merely relaying them (union representative).

> It's an engineers' company ... all top executives are basically baggy pants engineers. Some of them are not very good managers; they are engineers (manager).

HRD felt that it had to keep a low profile on many issues because it did not have the power to impose decisions on line managers.

> [HRD] tried not to grab a high profile in the sense that: "it's our job and we'll tell them what to do". That would have been a gross error (executive).

As a result, it was difficult for HRD to gain acceptance for alternative approaches to the problem of retrenchment.

> If human relations had been more powerful and management less control-oriented, then other alternatives might have been considered (JPC member).

This situation appeared to be changing to a certain extent. Ironically, the retrenchment program provided a good opportunity for HRD personnel to demonstrate their worth, particularly with their management of the outplacement program. Moves within the function itself were being made to try and improve its credibility in the company.

Also, a new executive vice-president, with an engineering background, had been appointed as head of HRD (and other departments). His support of HRD and his credibility as an engineer had helped to improve the status of the function.

> I think it made a difference putting in charge a senior manager who has come out of a major line function. I think it helped [HRD's] credibility (executive).

Moves such as these should help to place a higher emphasis on the human resource element of strategic thinking in the company and, perhaps, avoid some of the planning problems mentioned earlier.

The Outcome

What, then, was the outcome of AECL's retrenchment exercise? A total of 510 people were scheduled for layoff: 200 from the Society of Professional Engineers and Associates; 100 technical; 65 from the Public Service Alliance of Canada; and 145 Administrative (and a further 90 from a plant in Montreal). The total cost of the people who were laid off was $ 3.9 m – $ 7,100 per person. It included settlements, which ranged form $ 2,000 to $ 40,000, the cost of the committees, seminars, grievances, job searching, and redeployment.

There were about 120 grievances, of which 24 were resolved in favour of the grievor. Employee representatives on the Mississauga Joint Planning Committee (JPC) applied for and were granted arbitration on the terms of AECL's adjustment program. In the employees' view, however, the arbitrator was given unworkable terms of reference, and nothing of consequence resulted. The Montreal JPC went to arbitration on the basis that the severance terms discriminated on the basis of age. The solution proposed by the arbitrator was to take back the compensation and redistribute it. It pleased neither AECL nor the unions, and both parties agreed to reject the award.

The morale of continuing employees – a key issue if the company is to prosper in the 1980s – had been damaged. It was partly due to the precarious position of the industry. AECL subsequently announced another 500 layoffs in its Candu operations, as well as a reduction in research spending and the closure of two heavy water plants in Nova Scotia.

> It [retrenchment] has had a lasting effect on morale here. Up until a couple of years ago we were a high flying group of people, we were always growing. Everything that looked good doesn't look good any more (manager).

Some people, however, felt the company did not deal with the layoffs as well as it might have. They felt "let down and insecure".

> I suspect that, given the chance, about 80 per cent of the staff here would leave. If they got the chance of a job somewhere else, they would go right after it (union representative).

Having said that, it must be granted that AECL did an excellent job in managing a new and difficult problem, and that most employees, despite their criticisms, agreed.

> I think, given the extent of layoffs and the fact that the company had never used the [contract] language before, they did well (union representative).

The downsizing program failed to rectify immediately AECL's problems, and net income fell over 60 per cent between 1983 and 1984. An improvement was recorded over the following three years, with net income nearly 90 per cent higher in 1987 than in 1984, although it was still lower than in 1982. Employee numbers have fallen dramatically since 1982 and were 38 per cent lower in 1987 than in 1982.

Chapter 7: Air Canada

Air Canada is a large crown corporation which employs more than 22,000 people and supplies flights throughout Canada, the USA, and to many other parts of the world. It is the ninth largest airline in the International Air Transport Association group in terms of passenger-kilometres. Founded in 1937 as Trans Canada Air Lines, it has since grown in terms of number of aircraft, available seats, new destinations, and total route miles. Passenger transport is the focus of its operations, although it also carries mail and cargo.

1982 was not a good year for Air Canada: a $40 million profit in 1981 turned into a $32 million loss; return on investment dropped from 7 per cent to 1.7 per cent; and return on equity was a negative 6.4 per cent (figures from 1982 Annual Report). The loss was attributed to the "prevailing recessionary climate", which resulted in a decline in air traffic to 1977/8 levels. This situation made clear the need for some form of cutback, a process that had, to some extent, already been initiated.

> 1982 has been a testing year ... our financial results would have been much worse had we not begun several years ago to prepare ourselves for a decline in traffic and the intensified pressure of competition in the face of rising costs (Annual Report, 1982).

The outlook for the airline industry was not reassuring. The Air Transport Association of America predicted that American scheduled carriers would lose U.S. $400–500 million in 1982. They had already lost more than $400 million in 1981. Members of the International Air Transport Association lost more than U.S. $2 million in 1982. Many American airlines had already started to retrench. Transworld Airlines, Pan American, Eastern, Delta, among many others, had instituted salary freezes, deferrals, and reductions among all levels of employees. Continental Airlines declared itself bankrupt and filed for reorganization. Braniff Airlines had similar problems. The deregulation of the American airline industry was blamed for many of these difficulties, but it was, in effect, only exacerbating the underlying problems of recession and declining markets, coupled with rising costs and price competition.

Even without the (then) imminent threat of deregulation in Canada, Air Canada could not afford to ignore the plight of its American counterparts, particularly with relatively high labour costs at 37 per cent of total expenses. They were higher than many competitors including Continental, Pan Am, American, and, particularly, Peoples' Express which had labour costs of only 20 per cent.

> Other airlines do not organize many of their functions at the almost luxurious levels we were at (executive).

1982 signalled the need for an examination of how costs could be cut.

> As the Corporation adjusted to declining traffic levels, reductions have had to be made. Many Air Canada people are sharing jobs with fellow employees or contributing hours to enable others to stay employed. Reductions in both management and contract staff were forced by external circumstances. They were made after full and complete discussions with the unions representing our people, and through a voluntary separation program which allowed permanent reduction in management staffing (1982 Annual Report).

The aim was to reduce costs in the range of 10 to 15 per cent, which meant reducing human resource costs to 1977/78 levels: management by 15 per cent; unionized staff[1] by 8 per cent. Clerical staff numbers were considered satisfactory.

More than 1,000 employees were temporarily laid off, and the equivalent of another 300 jobs were reduced through worksharing. Employees in some units worked four days instead of five while receiving unemployment insurance contributions (UIC) for the fifth day, to bring income up to 91 per cent of previous levels. Pilots had agreed to work fewer hours with a cut of up to $ 6,000 in their annual salary. An early retirement package involving up to six months pay had been offered and accepted by some 60 members of different unions. Leaves of absence had also been agreed to. A voluntary separation offer was

[1] The unions include Canadian Airline Pilots' Association (CALPA), Canadian Airline Employees' Association (CALEA),Canadian Airline Flight Attendants' Association (CALFAA), the International Association of Machinists and Aerospace Workers (IAMAW). The latter did not negotiate any concessions to save jobs.

extended to all management levels and was taken up by more than 600 individuals. Following a hiring freeze, pay awards for managers were deferred for six months and, for senior managemerrt, one year. An employee suggestion program saved $ 860,000 in 1982. The overall result of these actions was:

> [a] major formal program of broad corporate restraint affecting management salaries, staff levels, flight schedules, pricing, capital expenditures, and operating expenses (1982 Annual Report).

The Voluntary Separation Program

This chapter focusses on the Voluntary Separation Program (VSP) that was offered to managers. On 30th August 1982, a letter was sent out to all management levels from the Vice-President (Personnel) announcing a voluntary separation package. All managers were eligible, qualifying for one months pay per year of service, up to a maximum of eighteen months. Those with less than three years eligible service would receive three months pay, those with less than three years to normal retirement were limited to half the remaining months.

Applicants could elect to receive these payments in any one or combination of methods: a lump sum cash payment; time on payroll; or "makeup" payments that would apply to the pension if retirement was before the age of sixty (two months of award equalled one year of "make up"). Normal retirement benefits and pensions applied. Employees were to be notified by the end of January 1983 if their application was successful, and were expected to leave by the end of April, although Air Canada could extend that date. Nearly 18 per cent of managers took advantage of the program, which resulted in more than 600 leaving the company.

The voluntary separation program was offered as a means of cutting costs on a permanent basis, as a contribution to the total of $ 50–60 million required by the company. The company needed about 500 volunteers. To achieve this, an incentive in the form of a generous settlement was deemed necessary.

> We are prepared to provide incentives where these will produce long-term savings. ... Thus, in the case of management, rather than simply

> identifying the 500 management jobs that must be eliminated, terminating the people in these jobs and making payments in lieu of notice equivalent to what the court would award, we are trying to seek 500 volunteers who would volunteer to resign or retire in place of the 500 who would normally be terminated. The amount of money that would ordinarily be paid to terminated managers in lieu of notice would instead be offered as an incentive (Vice-President (Personnel) quoted in company magazine).

Five hundred volunteers would produce a cost saving of about $12 million in 1984, and a somewhat larger amount in following years.

The scheme was voluntary in that no one was forced to resign, although subtle pressure was put on some employees, according to some managers. Air Canada reserved the right to approve applications depending on company needs for "certain skills, experience, management succession, continuity of company operations, concentrations of applications by Branch, Region location, etc." (the letter announcing the program). The company wanted to prevent the loss of certain skilled employees to other airline companies – not only would valued expertise be lost to the competition but, since they would have to be replaced, no cost saving would be made.

Employees who took advantage of the program received their due payments and benefits. There were some general sessions explaining the nature of the offer and providing information about savings plans and where to find financial advice. There was no pre-retirement counselling, outplacement aid, or specialist financial advice. Some exit interviews were held.

The Reasons

Why did Air Canada choose a voluntary program? It had led to a debate among senior executives, some of whom were concerned that "that the wrong people would go". Even though the company had the right of refusal, these managers felt it would be difficult to exercise it, given the size of the offer and peoples' expectations. Despite these reservations, however, the overall feeling was that selective dismissals would have been:

> out of keeping with our style of management, out of keeping with our CEO[2] and all he has talked about in the last 5 or 6 years about Air Canada being a team and a family (executive).

Previous cutbacks had been carried out in 1970. The chief executive officer (CEO) at the time had employed external consultants to effect the changes. They had carried them out with little regard for the employees concerned, and the result had been, according to many, complete chaos. Stories abounded, for example, about individuals arriving at work and finding someone else's name on their office.

> We haven't got over it yet, and you only have to mention the name of that consulting company 13 years later and people are sneering (executive).

The current CEO was, in contrast, an "airline man" and viewed by staff as a knowledgeable and compassionate individual, who had encouraged a "respect for the individual".

> That was the first thing [the CEO] said: we will not do it that way again (manager).

This new people-oriented culture had been nurtured by the management team. If cuts were not to jeopardize it, they would have to be "voluntary – as painless as possible".

> [A voluntary program] avoids the necessity of firing anyone and distributes the money which *the Company would have to pay anyway*, to volunteers who would be able to leave the Company voluntarily and with some additional advantages without hurting anyone. This, to me, is very consistent with Air Canada's people philosophies, operating principles, and style of management (VP (Personnel) quoted in company magazine).
>
> We have a culture here where we have a high degree of respect for individuals, so we were very reluctant to lay people off (manager).

The legal situation also had a major impact on the size of the severance terms. Courts were taking into account the difficulty of finding a new job and inflation when making their awards. The eighteen months of severance pay was in keeping with these awards.

---

[2] The chief executive officer and President has recently been promoted to Chairman of the Board. For the purposes of this report, however, he will continue to be referred to as CEO.

> This payment will be roughly equivalent to what the courts deem to be the amount of cash necessary to provide the individual with income until a similar position can be obtained elsewhere. In general, the courts have been awarding payments in the range of twelve to twenty-four months depending on service and level in the organization (VP (Personnel) quoted in company magazine).

> At that time they [the courts] were giving settlements that were pretty high. We had to go to eighteen months to obviate that problem, to be able to say we're giving what that person would get if we forced him to go to court (executive).

Air Canada wanted to ensure that its retrenchment policy did not raise public criticism and compromise its government stakeholders.

> The government has every right to expect their crown agencies to be exemplary in the way they deal with people (executive).

As a large and prominent state-owned organization, Air Canada attracts considerable media attention.

> We sometimes get a little sorry for ourselves because we feel we're such a beautiful target (executive).

A voluntary program reduced the risk of adverse publicity.

The fact that the program was voluntary led to a decision not to provide the extensive support measures seen in other organizations. Managers felt that, since people were choosing to leave and, for the most part, taking early retirement, there was no need for outplacement services.

> The point was that because the thing was voluntary there was no real need (manager).

> I guess the judgement was we'd done enough (human resource manager).

Facilitating Factors

What factors helped Air Canada carry out its retrenchment program? One factor was undoubtedly its experience with previous downsizing programs, in two respects. The earlier episode in 1970 had shown the company how *not* to do it. In addition, "gloom and doom files", containing the records of a 1977 early retirement scheme (taken up by 363 managers) provided the basic mechanisms for the current downsizing. As a result of these files, the company was able to put together its retrenchment program relatively quickly.

Guidance also came from the experiences of the U.S. airlines which had had to deal with the industry's problems a little earlier than Air Canada. Many of these companies had "just fired a gun", and provided another model of how not to handle retrenchment. The American situation also provided an indication of what would happen if Air Canada did not take action.

> We, seeing that [the U.S. situation] and realizing that we faced it, began, I guess in 1980, to think about how we were going to control our costs (executive).
>
> Comparing ourselves with other airlines, and that was our main thrust, we felt we probably were a little fat. We had this gut feeling that we were a little heavy, but the real impetus came with the comparison of other airlines (executive).

The early thinking prompted by the U.S. experience helped to avoid a last minute panic.

> It certainly wasn't a crisis situation; it was a recognition over several years that the economy wasn't going to turn around and save us, that we would have to take some action to get to grips with a generally declining economy (manager).

Senior management used this time to ensure that the need for cuts was accepted and understood throughout the organization. Preceding the retrenchment program was an audiovisual program called the "Air Canada Challenge". It included a film, talks with unions, articles in the company magazine, and face-to-face meetings with employees in which the situation of the company was explained.

> We were using every tool, every medium including face-to-face discussion to explain what was happening in our industry, what was happening to our costs, what was happening in the States, what deregulation was starting to do. ... We tried to tell them what was really difficult news and to give them a picture of what we were trying to do – the marketing efforts we were mounting, how gasoline was being saved, the money that was being spent on becoming more efficient. That was a kind of background for everybody in the company to say we've got to clamp down, we've got to squeeze, we've got to cut costs, increase productivity (executive).

The human resource (HR) function was a strong influence on the way in which the cutbacks were carried out because it had a relatively high status within the organization.

> I can think of a number of organizations where HR is a staff function, where the line is pretty autonomous, and staff is there to be called upon when, as, and if they are needed, and until then they keep quiet. That is a different kind of structure from here (manager).

The power of HR had increased with the current chief executive officer. The function was headed by a Senior Vice-President who sat on the President's Group of half a dozen key executives. "Power is not an issue", according to human resource managers. It was, as a result, relatively easy to justify the cost of the program to the senior management team.

The age distribution of the workforce helped Air Canada. The company's post-war commercialization and growth meant a great many relatively old, long-serving managers. In addition to providing large numbers of individuals who would benefit from voluntary severance, it also meant that the program appeared to be an early retirement scheme although, strictly speaking, it was not. Thus, the profile of the layoffs was lowered and the perceived need for support measures reduced.

The Outcome

How successful has Air Canada been? There have been some problems with the reorganization that accompanied the layoffs. At the time of the offer, unit managers were asked to identify their 20 per cent least essential positions (LEPs). If a LEP was vacated by a manager who was leaving as a result of voluntary separation, there was no problem. However, in many cases, "essential" posts were vacated, while managers were left in LEPs. These remaining managers had to be matched with the vacant positions. The resulting reorganization and retraining was a formidable task. It meant some leavers had to stay on after April 1983 to train their successors, while managers in LEPs sometimes had to wait six months before knowing where they would be moved. They then had to adjust to a new job.

> It took too long between the announcement that they were downsizing and the time it was done. People didn't know what they were doing, where they were going (employee).

Some individuals undoubtedly left as a result of having their position declared an LEP, since it meant there was no longer any certainty about what form their future career would take.

> The fact that my position was declared "least essential" and that I could not be advised as to my future (doing what and where) prompted my decision [to leave] (employee).

Another problem concerned the twenty or so people whose applications for voluntary severance were not approved. Some people were denied it because of their much needed technical skills. These denials raised considerable criticism. It is difficult to know exactly how big a problem the denials represented. Certainly, with only twenty individuals, it was on a relatively small scale, but it is worth noting that of the people approached in this particular group, none was willing to grant an interview.

The fact that a large number of people left the organization has not caused any major problems in terms of the loss of expertise or experience.

> A lot of people say nobody's indispensable and it seems to be true because I was quite afraid when I saw the number of people leaving and the quality of those people, but it turned out we could do without them (manager).

Instead, promotion opportunities have been opened up.

> [Losing good people] certainly hasn't crippled us because what it's done has provided opportunities for people who were waiting. So we haven't really suffered, even though we've lost a lot of experience (executive).

Such opportunities are particularly important in a time of contraction. With no expansion, younger individuals have limited career prospects and, given salary restraint, there are few other ways to reward and motivate them.

> I am a little bit concerned about those who stay because in a time of restraint it's "millions" for those who go and nothing for those who don't (executive).

The morale of the remaining managers appeared to be high. Interviewees expressed no feelings of bitterness. Employees appeared confident of their future with the company and its chief executive officer.

> I feel very confident that he's [the CEO] there ... [and] you feel more comfortable because you know they are going to look after their employees (employee).

No criticism was voiced about the lack of support measures.

> If someone has decided to take early retirement, I don't think they should expect the company to find them a part-time job (employee).

In summary, people felt that the company had treated them fairly.

> I think people were extremely well treated: the severance terms were very fair (employee).
>
> I believe this program is very generous and the people responsible should be commended (employee).
>
> Throughout my career I would like to state that AC is the finest company I have ever been associated with. It was a pleasure working for them (employee).

Management also felt that the voluntary separation program had, then, been a success.

> We generally feel we've accommodated their departure very well. On the one hand, we've lost experience. On the other, we gained fresh ideas and energy and have a new enthusiasm (manager).
>
> We had 600 basically smiling faces that went out the door (executive).

The program did give rise to some problems regarding the unions who represented nonmanagerial ranks. These employees did not qualify for such generous severance terms since their contracts protected them from permanent layoff. They are laid off temporarily and, when conditions permit, rehired. As a result, they did not qualify for the same payments as the managers who left permanently. Some of the union officials, particularly the International Association of Machinists and Aerospace Workers (IAMAW), which represented some 8,000 employees, did not accept the distinction between temporary and permanent layoffs. They refused to negotiate concessions and demanded, instead, a similar program. The result was a public fight as the IAMAW involved the media in what was known as the "Golden Finger Campaign", in which they criticized the company for unfairly discriminating between managerial and nonmanagerial ranks.

> Any kind of voluntary program that you don't give to them [the IAMAW] – they will feel discriminated against (manager).

The voluntary separation program can be considered, despite some problems, a success both in terms of how it was carried out and the cost savings that were achieved. Air Canada continued to be heavily engaged in retrenchment with concessionary contracts, wage restrictions, and additional severance programs in 1984 and 1985. The success of these measures has been mixed. Following the 1982 loss, profits were posted in 1983 and 1984. The following year once again saw a loss. More recent years seem to indicate that the company is on the way to recovery. Profits increased from $3 million in 1983 to $46 million in 1987, return on investment doubled to 8 per cent, return on equity increased fivefold – but is still less than some major competitors, such as British Airways and Transworld Airlines – and the number of employees increased slightly.

Currently, the major issue facing Air Canada has changed from retrenchment to privatization. Moves towards further deregulation in the Canadian airline industry are expected to create additional competitive pressures for Air Canada. The airline also requires new planes, which will cost as much as $2 billion dollars. Executives have, however, convinced the government to reduce its stake in the company as a means of increasing both its flexibility and access to resources in order to deal with these pressures. In October 1988, the government sold 45 per cent of its shares, with an assurance not to interfere in the running of the corporation, and certain conditions on foreign ownership and the size of individual stakes. The sale was strongly supported by Air Canada's management, but has been opposed by both opposition parties.

Chapter 8: Ville Marie

Ville Marie is a social service centre responsible, in effect, for the anglophone (English-speaking) population of Montreal. It is a government agency and responsible to the Ministère des Affaires Sociales (MAS) of Quebec. It employed approximately 650 individuals in the various areas of social welfare. In 1981, it was faced with budget cuts of 11 per cent, which represented a reduction of more than $ 2 million in the annual budget.

Ville Marie had been anticipating cuts for some time, but had been unaware of the exact magnitude. Consequently, managers had worked out three cutback scenarios, representing reductions of 8, 10, and 12 per cent. In July 1981, Ville Marie received notification from the ministry of the exact budget reduction it faced, and a request for a plan of how it was to be implemented. The board initially attempted to resist these reductions and passed a resolution to avoid cuts in direct services and concentrate, instead, on administrative costs. On the 8th September, a public meeting was held, inviting client and community groups to voice their opinions of Ville Marie and the proposed budget. The media were also invited. The consensus of this meeting was that the agency should refuse to accept the cuts. On the 10th September, the board decided against submitting the plan for the $ 2.3 million cutbacks and, instead, submitted a plan which incorporated a reduction of only $ 248,601 in administrative overheads. It was formally supported by the Clinical Staff Advisory Committee (CSAC – a staff – management committee) and informally by most managers, union officials, and employees.

The alternative plan listed a number of explanations for the refusal to comply with ministry directives. It argued that an 11 per cent cut would result in a loss of 84 positions which, in turn, would prevent Ville Marie from providing the services which, under its mandate, it was obliged to offer. Support from the community had indicated that these services were needed. Ville Marie also questioned the assumptions which underlay the ministry's calculation of its budget. It argued that, as one of the few anglophone institutions in the province, it was forced to provide services to anglophones who lived outside its catchment area. Consequently, its target population was considerably larger than that assumed and financed by the ministry.

A meeting was set up between the minister and representatives of Ville Marie to discuss the agency's position, but to no avail. A press release from the chairman of the board on the 14th October stated that the minister was unresponsive to the request for more funds, and was still demanding an 11 per cent cut. On 27th October 1981, a new plan was submitted, which complied with this demand.

This plan was implemented during November and December. The necessary actions had already been worked out by senior management, as a result of their scenario planning, and local managers were left to put them into effect. The resulting layoffs and "bumpings"[1] were all completed by December 24th 1981. Ministry guidelines assigned ranges of permissible cuts to the different programs. Within these ranges, management implemented cuts very much in an across-the-board fashion.

A Resource Allocation Methodology Committee (RAM) had been set up to establish acceptable criteria on the basis of which priorities could be set and resources allocated. It had had limited success, however, because of the lack of sophisticated data and analysis. Moreover, a period of fiscal constraint was not considered the ideal time in which to introduce complex and controversial new planning procedures.

> I don't think the organization was psychologically prepared to get into that type of accounting and budgeting approach. I think there was a problem of maintaining power bases in the organization, and, to a great extent, we didn't have the necessary systems to provide the data to do that type of analysis (central manager).

With hindsight some managers felt that, because of the resource reduction, there was, in fact, a need for acceptable criteria to legitimize differential resource allocation.

---

[1] An individual whose post is closed has the right to "bump" other employees with less seniority. The individual's first move is to bump the person with least seniority in that centre of activity. This person then bumps whoever is next on the seniority list from the other centres of activity. This process is repeated until the person with least seniority is reached – that person is the one to lose his/her job. Some constraints are placed on bumping: it must be the same job title, i. e., counsellor, social worker, staff, and it has to be within the same bargaining unit.

> If you don't have the sophisticated procedures, then you're back to value judgements, and you could have ten different people with ten different value judgements (divisional manager).

Ville Marie, however, decided to opt out of making difficult selective decisions and, instead, cut across the board within the confines of ministry guidelines. Senior management was reluctant to implement selective cuts for fear of a political backlash by local managers.

> We were trying to apply the cuts across-the-board so that nobody would be hurt too much (board member).

Ville Marie had been formed by amalgamating various private institutions, which had been incorporated into the social service centre as separate divisions or centres of activity. Many of the division directors continued to think in terms of "their" division, rather than of Ville Marie as a whole.

> Ville Marie is a conglomerate of different places and each has a different history, therefore a different way of looking at things (employee).

> We're still very much decentralized in the way that we have three major areas. So you get a group of managers that say: Why her more than me or why him more than me? On what basis are you doing it, and we haven't been satisfied with the tools you've come up with. So what we decided to do was say: "Let's take a percentage cut across the board". So we did (central manager).

It was felt that selective cuts would result in divisional managers trying to "protect their turf".

> As a manager you want to protect jobs. You also want to protect what you are doing – we all want to protect our own hide, there's no doubt about it (divisional manager).

The Process

There were, in effect, two processes occurring at the same time: there was both the attempt to resist the cuts, and the decision-making process about where the cuts should be made. The unions had been involved in the public campaign against the cuts. They were, however, excluded from the process of deciding where and how the cuts should be implemented. Most of these decisions were being taken by senior management as a result of its scenario planning. Despite discussions between management and union representatives, the latter felt that the managers were playing "their cards very close to their chests".

> We felt at that time we were being played with, that there were always hidden agendas we were not aware of ... we felt manipulated ... we would get a document but we wouldn't know its history, wouldn't know its true purpose. There were attempts to con CSAC into approving things without being given the full information (CSAC [Clinical Staff Advisory Committee] representative).

Union officials and employees argued that they wanted more information sharing, but they did not expect, nor did they want, the responsibility for decision making. They felt that it was not their job to participate in decisions which could result in fellow employees being laid off.

> We're not going to help managers make the cuts – that's management's job (union representative).

They maintained that their concern revolved around a lack of information which, they believed, reflected a lack of competence on the part of central management.

> The lack of a clear management strategy to implement the cutbacks was the main source of our anxiety ... the unions feared a plan that would cut more posts than necessary, more dislocation via bumping ... we suspected that the cutbacks had produced a kind of paralysis among senior management and we did not perceive them to be working well as a team (union representative).

Another criticism resulted from the perception that senior management was trying to save management posts at the expense of line staff. The protection of managerial jobs was not considered to be legitimate, since representatives felt that the social workers were already overloaded. Unions also felt that managers were trying to protect managerial perks and fringe benefits, while the staff were "scraping the barrel" [doing as much as they could] to make cuts.

> Social workers live with a high degree of personal stress which cannot be judged any more or less than that of the administrators of the system. Why should one group have certain protections over another in the rhetoric of "We're all in this together" (union representative).

Interviewees, unanimously, believed that there was a proliferation of "dead wood" in central management and that managers were, unjustifiably, trying to spare themselves from the cutbacks.

> I think people got discouraged that not many people were cut in management levels. They said so many managers were cut, and then we still see them around. ... I think there's a lot of dead wood around and it wouldn't hurt to stir it up a little (employee).

The unions were torn between their desire not to jeopardize the campaign against the budget reductions by publicly confronting management, and their concern about layoffs. At first, they tried a low-profile approach with closed-door negotiations with management about how the cuts would be made. When that failed, they took a more public stand criticizing management and instituting a computer boycott[2]. There actions developed into a confrontation between management and unions.

> Management was trying to fight for the right to distribute funds as they saw fit ... the unions were fighting for jobs (board member).

Management was angry with the unions because they felt the public questioning of management expenses would jeopardize the campaign to prevent the cuts.

> The board and management were very disappointed at one point because they [the unions] wanted information that I don't think should be made public because it can be misconstrued. They used a lot of that information and tried to embarrass management and the board. ... They used that information in bad faith in my estimation (board member).

Nevertheless, the stand taken by the unions did put some pressure on management to focus more on administrative expenses, rather than cutting line personnel.

> I don't know whether the board would have stood so solidly on the side of cutting administration as opposed to services if the unions hadn't done what they did (central manager).

Information sharing also appeared to be a problem at the local level, when the cuts were being implemented. Many managers felt it was inappropriate to release too much information, for fear of worrying employees.

---

[2] Employees have to enter various statistics on the computer for the benefit of the ministry. By boycotting the computer, they were effectively refusing to do the "paperwork".

> I made up my mind that I wasn't going to impart any information, no matter how definitely it was presented, until it actually came to the point that we'd made the decision. Then you do have more information than, in fact, you're giving out, and employees know that and they resent it. It's a form of paternalism or parentalism – keeping back that information because it's going to hurt you (divisional manager).

> You can add to anxiety if, before you even know anything, you go and start talking to staff saying we're going to have so much of a cutback (divisional manager).

This paternalistic attitude was severely criticized. The majority of interviewees argued that they were social workers, who were not going to "fall apart at the seams" [be unable to cope] at receiving this kind of information.

> If they had even an inkling, we should still be part of it, and I feel we're adults and we're able to cope with this kind of information (union representative).

Union representatives voiced the complaint that they wasted a lot of time trying to find out information on the cuts. They felt they could have used this time much more productively by helping the people who were to be bumped or laid off. In the absence of concrete information, rumour prevailed, which was inevitably worse than the reality.

> It was mostly rumour. That's what we found so maddening – that there was nothing we could grasp. It was just rumour and it was very tense. Everyone was concerned that they might be cut, and they didn't know whether it was going to be by seniority or not (employee).

Employees felt that the most pessimistic scenario would have been better than letting everyone worry; it would have enabled people to plan. One individual, for example, expecting to be laid off since she was a recent recruit, moved to a smaller apartment and started saving money in anticipation of this.

On the whole, employees who were laid off or bumped appreciated the way in which they were dealt with by management, particularly by those managers who took the extra trouble to deliver the news personally.

> It was nice of [the divisional director] to give it to us personally and not in an inter-office memo (employee).

The complaints that were made revolved around hearing news about bumping or layoffs from colleagues, rather than the appropriate manager and not being given the news in a sensitive or sympathetic way.

The bumping process left its scars. It resulted in people with specialized skills, qualifications, and experience being moved to jobs where they were no longer appropriate. It also meant leaving a group of friends and joining a new team, which had seen its original member "ousted" by the newcomer. These changes upset social groups and often led to resentment and uneasy working relationships. Virtually all interviewees had a "horror story" to tell.

> The whole concept of bumping is professionally repugnant and very personal. ... There are still grudges borne. ... You have choices, and so it all gets very personal – why did you bump me? (employee).

Employees also felt that the cuts had resulted in increased work loads and reductions in some services. Interviewees complained of longer waiting lists and certain programs being virtually destroyed. Many line staff talked of increased stress, disillusionment, and "burn out" as a result of heavier case loads.

The Fight Against the Cuts

Ville Marie's attempt to resist the cuts was ultimately unsuccessful. It also caused a number of problems for the members of the agency. First, by delaying the cuts, the magnitude of the eventual reductions in staff may have been increased, since the budget still had to be balanced at the end of the year. Second, the action sent contradictory messages to employees. On the one hand, the board was saying that the cuts must be resisted. On the other hand, management were busy preparing the three scenarios so that it could implement the cuts as swiftly and as effectively as possible.

> It we do have to cut, then we had better be ready for it – otherwise we're going to lose another month or two months or three, and we're going to be in a right mess then (central manager).

Consequently, many employees were unsure as to exactly what management's plans were.

> At the same time the board had a firm position that they weren't going to make cuts, management was busy piling up how cuts were going to be made. There was a public stonewalling at the same time as we were working away on how you go and do it. That caused distrust from the staff who felt that the process was going on anyway, even though, officially, it was not (local manager).

Third, in presenting a "deserving case" to the public and ministry, the worst picture was painted to create support, sympathy, and legitimacy. This information obviously reached the staff, amongst whom it caused a great deal of anxiety. The original objection to the cuts was made on the basis that 84 posts would have to be closed. Because of attrition, however, only 22 people were actually laid off.

Fourth, the awkward position in which the union found itself contributed to tensions between management and employees. Union representatives had to support actions which might prevent the cuts while, at the same time, they felt they were being excluded from the process of deciding where the cuts would be made. This situation helped lead to the confrontation between central management and unions discussed earlier.

There are a number of reasons why the attempt to prevent cutbacks ultimately failed. One argument was that Ville Marie was simply not powerful enough.

> We are not a big power block in the ministry. The big boys are the hospitals, and if the hospitals can't influence them, then we didn't have much hope (central manager).

Joint action with the other Montreal social service centres might have improved Ville Marie's chances of success. Although there was some communication between Ville Marie and Montréal Métropolitain (the francophone social service agency), no united action took place. Montréal Métropolitain is considerably larger than Ville Marie and, as such, is relatively more powerful.

Ville Marie consciously chose to act alone, fighting the cuts on the basis of protecting anglophone social services. It has been argued that, politically, it was an untenable strategy in a predominantly French-speaking province.

> You're fighting a losing battle – there's no way they're going to exempt the anglophone agency and allow all the francophone agencies to absorb their cuts (central manager).

On the other hand, it has been argued that a united resistance campaign was infeasible since the two agencies were, effectively, competing for the same funds.

> Cooperation tends to break down because everyone is competing for their share of the same pie within the region of Montreal (divisional manager).

The result was that, by itself, Ville Marie had little leverage with which to deal with the government. When the ministry refused to accept its arguments, there was little the agency could do. Had they objected further, they would have run the risk of being put into trusteeship.

Another problem with the resistance campaign was the lack of quantitative data it could marshall to support its arguments. The attempt to demonstrate that the government had underestimated the social service needs of the anglophone population was unsuccessful because Ville Marie failed to provide "objective" criteria to "prove" its case. Ville Marie was inexperienced in this type of political strategy and simply had not collected or prepared the appropriate data. It did not have the necessary figure or sufficient political expertise to use them.

> We are not preparing those numbers, they [the ministry] were, and when you sit down to argue the budget you argue numbers: we didn't have those numbers. ... We'd sit down at budget-arguing time with very little data to prove out point. We knew we were getting shortchanged but we couldn't substantiate that with quantifiable data (board member).

The minister, on the other hand, "played with figures and bombarded us with new statistics which were not made available to us for examination" (press statement made by Chairman of the Board, October 14, 1981).

Given the problems with the resistance campaign and its apparent lack of success, opinion was divided as to whether it was a worthwhile strategy. Some employees and union officials felt it was "schizophrenic" and "not terribly helpful". Others disagreed, arguing the cuts might have been worse and pointing to the fact that the public's awareness of Ville Marie and the destructive effect of government policies were raised.

> Basically, it didn't change a damn thing in relation to the money we had cut, but it certainly sensitized the public to the reality of Ville Marie. It certainly set the Minister thinking a bit (central manager).

Others have argued that it was important for the staff that management was seen to take a stand.

Summary and Conclusions

Ville Marie was relatively successful in implementing the cutbacks. Despite the initial tension between unions and managers, relations have recovered and, in fact, benefitted.

> I was impressed, I must say, by the way the unions handled [the cutbacks] and cooperated and worked very closely with us to make sure the effect of the bumping was minimal (divisional director).
>
> It's a better management team now. It's a more knowledgeable management team. I think they're brighter (union member).

Consultation has been extended with the establishment of the Employee Relations Committee (ERC) which was designed, as a result of the problems that occurred around the budget cuts, to deal with issues which fall outside of the normal communication channels. The ERC was perceived as a significant achievement by all groups.

> There's nothing to hide. That's the attitude we're taking with the ERC. Look, we're all in this together. There are certain decisions that management will make and whether you like it or not we'll make them, but you'll be informed and given the reasons (central manager).
>
> That's something we've worked out due to the last cuts. We worked out an arrangement for an ERC where the unions have to be involved. It's part of an agreement – all the unions plus management. In the future hopefully that will work (union representative).

Ville Marie continued to face external problems in the form of government proposals to reorganize social services in Quebec, which threatened to reduce its funding base, and result in the transfer of nearly one-half of its staff to other agencies. It would appear that Ville Marie has learnt from its experiences in 1981, and has been much better organized to fight these government proposals. The agency has forged close relations with the English rights group – Alliance Quebec – in its attempts to secure funding for providing services to all Montreal anglophones, even those outside its catchment area. It has also cooperated with Montréal Métropolitain in a bid to prevent the transfer of personnel from the social service centres to other agencies. In so doing, Ville Marie has continued to play a numbers game by arguing that only 22 posts are appropriate for transfer, as compared with over 200 posts indicated by the ministry. So far, the agency appears to have been successful, and there has been no significant reallocation of posts in Montreal.

Chapter 9: Midville

The next two chapters deal with hospital closures in the British National Health Service (NHS). The administrative system and procedures of the NHS are complicated and will therefore be briefly explained before the case studies are examined.

Following the 1974 reorganization[1] of the NHS, a number of distinct managerial levels were created (see *diagram 3*). The Department of Health and Social Security (DHSS) and its Secretary of State hold formal responsibility for the NHS. Immediately under the Secretary of State is a Minister of Health. Below this level are 14 Regional Health Authorities (RHA). They have between 18 and 24 members and a chairman, all of whom are appointed by the Secretary of State. The Regional Health Authority is responsible for a number of Area Health Authorities (AHA). Each has between 18 and 33 members including 1 consultant, 1 general practitioner, 1 university nominee, 1 trade unionist, 2 health service employees, a number of lay members (all of which are appointed by the Regional Health Authority) and local authority members (who make up at least one-third and are nominated by the local council to which they have been elected). The Area Health Authority is the decision-making body for the area – it responds to and votes on recommendations made by its managers. The Area Team of Officers (ATO) comprises the management team with the responsibility for strategic policy and planning. It does not have direct control over, but is supposed to liase with, the District Management Teams (DMT), which have responsibility for the operational management and day-to-day running of the districts into which the area is divided. In some cases, there is only a single district and the two functions of the Area Team of Officers (ATO) and District Management Team and merged under the Area Management Team (AMT). Consensus management was also introduced in 1974.

[1] The structure of the NHS is now different. Both chapters refer to the situation introduced by the 1974 reorganization.

Diagram 3: The Administrative Structure of the NHS

Department of Health and Social Security
Secretary of State for Health and Social Security
Minister of State for Health

Regional Health Authority

Area Health Authority

Area Team of Officers — District Management Team

In the event of a proposed closure, the usual procedure is for the District Management Team to recommend to the Area Team of Officers that a closure is justified on certain grounds. A proposal is then submitted to the AHA and, if the decision is affirmed, a consultative document is produced. This document should include the reasons for the closure, the disposal or alternative use of the site, the relationship between the closure and other developments in the area, and the implications for patients. This document is then circulated to unions, Community Health Councils (CHCs), local authorities, staff organizations, and advisory committees. At the same time, local members of Parliament, the RHA and the Department of Health and Social Security are informed and a press statement issued. Most of these groups are expected to make comments which the AHA is supposed to take into account when making its decision.

The opinion of the CHC is particularly significant. Each district has its own CHC, which is responsible for promoting and protecting the interests of the patients. If it objects to a closure and submits an alternative plan, the AHA must take it into account. If the AHA still wishes to proceed, it must refer the decision up to the RHA. If the RHA will not accept the CHC's proposals, then it must seek the approval of the Secretary of State who may or may not confirm the decision to close. Thus the CHC has a formal mechanism whereby it can register its objections. If, on the other hand, the CHC agrees to the closure, then the AHA can go ahead with it.

For more details on the National Health Service see, for example, Barnard (1974), The Royal Commission on the National Health Service (1976–9), and Hunter (1980).

Introduction to Midville

This chapter concerns the closure of "Withybrook" hospital by "Midshire" AHA. Withybrook was a small hospital some ten miles from "Midville" – a rapidly expanding market town in one of the Midland counties in England. Midshire AHA comprised two districts, one of which covered Midville and its surrounding districts. The other covered the remaining towns in the county.

Withybrook was originally a tuberculosis (TB) hospital, but with the virtual eradication of the disease, it catered for chest patients and "cold surgery" (varicose veins, vasectomies etc). It had the appearance of a small cottage hospital with attractive buildings in an idyllic country setting. According to one doctor, patients used to enjoy going there because it was small, friendly, and picturesque, and because they were not really ill – either undergoing minor surgery or convalescing. Its medical usefulness, however, was limited because of the lack of support facilities and its distance from the district general hospital (DGH) in town.

The AHA's policy had been to concentrate services at the general hospital, which had been greatly enlarged in recent years. A rationalization process was under way, and two geriatric units and a convalescent hospital had already been closed and their services transferred to the district general hospital. This process was, however, being accelerated due to the AHA's financial difficulties.

Over the years, NHS funds had not been distributed evenly, and disparities had grown up between the resources of different regions. Midshire was part of a region which, hitherto, had attracted funds, and was one of the richer regions. The government set up the Resource Allocation Working Party (RAWP) to devise a new formula to rectify the imbalances and distribute funds more fairly between the regions. As a result, the region of which Midshire was a part lost funds. The problem, however, from Midshire's viewpoint was that it had always been an underfunded area within the region by as much as £1 million per annum, according to area managers. With the loss of money through the new formula and the general economic stringency, which had resulted from government expenditure cuts in the mid-1970s, Midshire's small share was coming from an even smaller budget. This situation was exacerbated by Midshire's obligation to cater for 50 per cent of the population of a nearby new town until its own hospital was built.

In response to the general principle of rationalization and the need to save money, the District Management Team (DMT) recommended the closure of Withybrook in April 1977. It argued that the loss of beds would be compensated for by the opening of a new phase at the district general hospital although there would be a time lag of around two years. The AHA accepted the recommendation and proposed that a consultative document be prepared. In July 1977, the AHA accepted the document which then went out for consultation. In August, there was formal notice of the proposed closure.

The Community Health Council (CHC) called a public meeting in November and, as a result of the strength of feeling there, opposed the closure. It was supported by district and parish councils in the area, but not by Midville town or borough councils. The Confederation of Health Service Employees (COHSE), the main union at Withybrook, "deplored" the proposed closure. The CHC then made a formal objection to the DHSS. In December 1977, the AHA reaffirmed the decision to proceed with the closure, but, because of the CHC's action, had to pass the decision up to the RHA. The region supported the plan to close and passed the matter up again – to the Department of Health and Social Security. In March 1979, the Secretary of State accepted the closure. The matter, however, was not finished there – the new Conservative government, elected in May of that year, wanted to reconsider the closure. It was not until September that its approval was finally given.

Managerial Strategies

The main strategy was one of consultation with everyone involved in or affected by the closure. The key managerial figure in this was the chairman of the Area Health Authority (AHA) – Alan Dale. He led many of the discussions, making himself available for consultation with all of the various interest groups. He was able to draw on his experience not only with the health service, with which he had been involved for twenty-five years, but with the local council. When he took the AHA chairmanship in 1974, he was member of the local council and so was able to capitalize on both his standing as a public figure and his political contacts. He was also in a position to apply to Withybrook the lessons he had learnt from the previous three closures undertaken by the AHA.

Dale's doctrine was to "go and meet the people". One of the ways he did so was to attend the public meeting, called in November 1977, to explain the reasons behind the closure. Consultation with the unions and the CHC was also extensive.

> There was full consultation with everybody, including the unions. There were lots of meetings. We told staff rather than let them read it in the papers. This is a general policy (manager).

As a result of this approach, both these groups felt that they had been fully consulted, and that they had been free to contact management should any problems arise.

> Relations are very good here. We are told informally: "Look out – in a month so and so's going to happen" (union official).
>
> We couldn't have faulted management – they spoke to everyone (union official).

Dale's strategy was supported by both the Area Team of Officers and the District Management Team. Both area and district administrators were convinced of the need for consultative management. As a result, management was perceived by other groups to be handling the closure in a respectable and fair way: in a legitimate manner.

Another group that was involved in this process was the doctors. If they had opposed the decision, they would have been able to mobilize considerable support, because they were perceived to be the experts by the public and the lay members of the AHA. In this case, however, they were offered new wards at another hospital, and there was no medical objection to the closure.

> Medical opinion is very influential. It would have made life difficult if they had all been against the closure (manager).

Redundancy payments were fixed by national agreements and, so, managers were unable to offer increased terms to secure goodwill. Instead, they offered everyone the choice between redundancy with compensation, and redeployment in a comparable job, where efforts were made to ensure that working conditions, shifts, hours, etc. were the same as those of their job at Withybrook. Many staff were very appreciative of having been given this choice.

> Management was very good about it. They gave people the choice of redundancy or a job (employee).
>
> All the staff were lucky. They had the choice of taking redundancy or another job (employee).

Another part of management's strategy involved emphasizing the necessity of the closure in the light of Midshire's financial position. The closure was presented as a financial imperative, even though there were other reasons why it took place.

> I know darn well that, had we had the money, we still would have closed it. They [the unions and the CHC] don't realise that. We were using the financial argument but what we were really after was rationalization (manager).

The financial argument, however, was easy to demonstrate to the potential opposition groups, who were already well aware that the area was grossly underfunded. The closure was, as a result, accepted as a means of saving desperately needed cash by the AHA, the unions, the CHC, and employees.

> I never had any fear of the AHA changing its mind ... they were haunted by the fear of overspending (Dale).
>
> There was no real opposition to the closure in the AHA, given the need to save money (AHA member).
>
> There was a good financial case for closure (union official).
>
> They just had not got the money to keep it going (employee).
>
> The staff knew there wasn't the money (steward).

Even the CHC "while opposing it in principle, was very understanding of the authority's problems" (manager). The rationalization argument, on the other hand, might have been less successful in convincing people of the need to close since there were conflicting medical opinions regarding the benefits of large integrated hospitals.

The Reasons

There were two main reasons for Midville's particular approach to closure. First, the area had had a history of good employee relations, which management was anxious to preserve. Consultation and an open process was considered an integral part of any strategy to preserve these working relationships.

> I've always believed that if you shy away from trade unions you have problems – so keep a working relationship (manager).

A second reason was the need to ensure that the closure could be implemented, even if the CHC opposed it and passed the decision up to the ministerial level. It had been expected that the CHC would register a formal protest – it had already opposed two of the previous three closures.

> They had to take up causes, and here was a cause that they could take up in a big way (manager).

If the CHC opposed the closure, the decision would be taken out of the area's hands. The support from the AHA and the RHA was not in question, but the involvement of the government added considerable uncertainty to the outcome. A spate of hospital occupations[2] during the mid-1970s had embarrassed the government; if a similar backlash had looked likely at Midville, the recommendation to close might well have been overturned. The chairman of the AHA tried to avoid this situation by handling the closure in such a way as to minimize the chances of confrontation.

> I thought that there was a good chance of this closure being accepted by the minister. The case was well made out, the local opposition was understandable, and there was no real threat of the union behaving in such a way that would embarrass the government. In other words, I couldn't see it becoming a conflagration. I could see it being a difficulty which someone had to grasp (chairman).

To increase the chances of approval, the chairman "took the battle over personally" (manager). He saw the relevant ministers in both governments and used his political experience to convince them of the need for closure.

---

[2] Situations where doctors, nurses, and ancillary workers unite to keep a hospital running in spite of managerial decisions to close it.

Even with this political intervention, and having reduced the chances of overt opposition, managers felt they were fortuitous in their timing. As the Conservatives took office in 1979, a policy began to emerge for the support of small community hospitals – like Withybrook.

> Dr Vaughan, Conservative Secretary of State for Health and Social Security ... suggests that the number of closures will be slowed by reducing the size of new DGHs and concentrating on "making the best of what exists" (The Guardian, 4th June 1980, p. 17).

The view among managers was that it would have been much more difficult to obtain approval for the closure, had it occurred much later. They felt that "the closure business is getting more difficult" (manager).

> If that proposal had come forward two years later, it would have had little chance of success (chairman).
>
> If it happened today, I doubt if we'd have got it through (manager).

At the time that the Conservatives had to consider the Withybrook closure, however, they had just fought an election on the basis of a cost-conscious manifesto. One of the ministers involved in the NHS was a recent recruit from Labour and, although a member of Parliament in the area, it is thought that he was anxious to be seen by his new party to be doing his duty – the affirmation of the closure of Withybrook was a chance to demonstrate that he and the new government meant business in cutting costs.

The Outcome

The outcome was largely successful for management, although a delay of eighteen months was incurred while approval was sought from the two successive governments. Nevertheless, they did manage, eventually, to close Withybrook. The unions, the CHC, and many employees had few complaints about the way in which management had handled the closure.

> Management handled it very well indeed. We have no complaints (union official).
>
> Everyone was very happy about the way it was managed (steward).

There was, however, some bitterness on the part of employees who lived in the village in which Withybrook was situated and who found it difficult to find other convenient work.

> We're retiring because we don't want to go anywhere else. We'd have problems working elsewhere in any case because there are no buses to [Midville] from where we live (ex-employee quoted in local paper, September 1979).
>
> As far as we know there are no jobs. They will offer you a job yes, but we have staff here from local villages. How the hell are they going to get into [Midville] (ex-employee quoted in local newspaper, October 1979).

Management achieved this success not only by providing mechanisms, such as compensation and consultation, to help employees deal with the change, but by adopting a political approach that took into account *all* interest groups, including the AHA, the CHC, the public, and the government. The chairman's view was that by being prepared for opposition, he was in a better position to deal with it. His aim had been to (a) assess the extent and nature of opposition, (b) to assess whether it would spread further than the local resistance expected in a hospital closure, and (c) if it were likely to spread, what were the implications and how powerful would the opponents be. This type of stance is particularly crucial in the public sector where accountability, ambiguous goals and government intervention make politics a fact of life.

Summary: Balancing Economic and Political Pressures

The five organizations discussed in this section were different compared to the first three companies. They, too, were aware of the political dimension of retrenchment but they were also constrained by a variety of economic factors. These constraints meant that they were in the difficult position of having to balance both economic and political pressures.

Andersons was concerned about the political repercussions of the closure because of the great potential for opposition from the unions and employees. Employeees at the plant had a reputation for militancy – 4 per cent and 18 per cent of available hours had been lost due to industrial action in 1976 and 1977. The factory was located in an area which had been associated with a number of factory occupations in the early 1970s. Local stewards had secured pledges of support from other British factories and, so, the prospect existed for local opposition to escalate into a companywide strike. The company also had to deal with some pressing economic constraints. The loss of over U.S. $ 200 million in 1978 had put the company in a precarious financial situation, and the increasing nervousness of investors had put pressure on management to find a way to reduce overhead and improve the company's balance sheet. Andersons also had little time in which to prepare for the news of job losses. So, on the one hand, political pressures dictated a gradual rundown and saving as many jobs as possible; while, on the other, economic forces were demanding decisive and drastic action.

The strategy of U.K. managers was to try and save some jobs in a variety of ways. They first tried to transfer production to the Scottish factory. They then conducted an international search to find a buyer for the factory and equipment. It proved unsuccessful, but a local work search indicated a demand for the engineering skills of the employees. So, the company helped set up a small subcontracting firm on the site of the original factory, providing jobs for around 200 employees. Managers also embarked on an extensive dialogue with unions to explain the reasons behind the closure, and provided redundancy compensation. These mechanisms were designed to induce the unions to adopt a peaceful route in two ways. First, by demonstrating that opposition would only cost them jobs and, second, by making sure that the company did not inadvertently make any procedural errors that might alienate the unions.

AECL managers were conscious of the political pressures associated with being a crown corporation. They were anxious to avoid undue adverse publicity which might provoke awkward political questions. They were also aware of the difficulties their employees would experience in dealing with layoffs. Many professional employees were involved who had previously been immune to redundancies and who would find it difficult to adjust to this new state of affairs and find new jobs in the depressed industry. AECL also had to accommodate economic constraints, in particular the loss of specialized skills which it considered crucial to the future success of the streamlined operation. A second constraint was cost: a voluntary program was initially ruled out because of the additional funds, which senior management felt would have been necessary to provide a sufficiently attractive incentive for people to leave. A third pressure was the lack of time to prepare, with declining market conditions following on so quickly from a boom economy.

As a result of economic concerns, the decision was made to select individuals for redundancy and, thus, keep critical skills in the organization. To help those who lost their jobs, compensation was paid and an extensive outplacement operation put into effect. Committees were set up to involve employees and to deal with specific outplacement needs and grievances.

Air Canada was also sensitive to political pressures. Like AECL, managers wished to avoid adverse publicity on the handling of the layoffs that would raise awkward political questions. They were also anxious to protect employee relations, since layoffs carried out under a previous administration in the early 1970s had provoked considerable criticism. The arrival of the new Chief Executive Officer in the mid-1970s had led to a change in the culture and a desire to improve and protect employee relations. In addition to these political considerations, Air Canada also saw itself facing one key economic constraint: the loss of people with key skills to the competition.

Since management was unwilling to compromise the new human relations philosophy with enforced dismissals, it offered a completely voluntary program. Restrictions were, however, placed on eligible employees, and the company reserved the right to refuse some applications. While there was an effort to keep these refusals to a minimum, some people (around 20) were not able to take advantage of the program. Severance pay of up to eighteen months salary was provided. The cost of this program was not considered a problem for the company, since it could be demonstrated that it would be recouped by the reduction in managerial overheads. Outplacement aid was not considered necessary because the program was voluntary, and most of the people were, in effect, taking early retirement and so were not looking for other work.

Ville Marie initially ran into problems with its unions and employees, who did not feel they were being adequately consulted. Subsequent actions suggest that management eventually started to appreciate this political dimension of the cutbacks and realized that employee/union acceptance was crucial to the successful implementation of cutbacks. The social service agency was also subject to economic constraints, since the minister had refused to accept their arguments, and their budget had to be balanced by the end of the fiscal year. Management's attempt to resist the cutbacks had exacerbated the time constraints by delaying the implementation of the cutbacks. As a result, the layoffs were made according to seniority which meant that most people did not qualify for redundancy pay because they had not been there long enough. Employee morale and union acceptance seem to have been protected, however, with the use of extensive consultation and communication.

Midville managers were acutely aware of a number of interest groups that could have opposed the closure. Managers could only make a recommendation for the closure. The actual decision had to be taken by the Area Health Authority (AHA), which represented a number of different constituencies. One of the more powerful groups was the local councillors, which made up one-third of the membership. These individuals were elected in local elections and, as a result, were often susceptible to public opinion. Consequently, public outcry at a proposed closure could translate into a large block of the AHA voting against management. In addition, the Community Health Council (CHC) could have taken the decision out of the hands of the AHA and pushed it up to the Secretary of State. Cabinet ministers were (and are) influenced by a very different constituency. Hospital occupations during the mid-1970s had already embarrassed the government. Had one been threatened at Midville, management felt that ministerial approval would have been unlikely. The interaction of all these different groups made the hospital closure a very political process. At the same time, however, managerial actions were constrained by national policies on redundancy, compensation, and union negotiations. In addition, the £1 million deficit put considerable financial pressure on the area.

The first step taken to avoid resistance was extensive consultation. Management also offered all employees of the hospital the choice between redundancy with compensation or a new job with the same conditions (e.g., hours, shifts, type of patient, etc.) as far as it was possible. These actions built credibility for management, providing an indication that they were trying to do the best they could for their employees, and with respect to the unions. Management was careful not to antagonize the doctors and offered them, in compensation, new wards in another hospital. In summary, although the CHC opposed the closure and sent the decision up to the minister, other groups did not intervene, and management was able to maximize the chances of approval.

The five organizations discussed in this section faced political pressures, which they had to accommodate with considerably less room for maneuvre than ICI, CIL, or Whitefields. Constraints in the form of time, dependency on key skills, cash reserves, or financial performance meant that managers had to balance economic and political concerns. Midville, perhaps, provides the clearest indication of how political retrenchment can become and, also, how the political constituencies can be successfully managed. The following chapter provides a useful comparison. It illustrates the dangers of underestimating the political implications of closing a hospital, to the extent that the attempt failed because of opposition from the various stakeholders.

I.3 Ignoring Political Pressures

Chapter 10: Northville

This chapter documents the ultimately unsuccessful attempt to close a maternity hospital known here as "Maine Road Maternity Hospital" by the Area Health Authority of a city in the northwest of England, known here as "Northville AHA".

Maine Road had been a candidate for closure since the 1960s simply because it was an old hospital. Following the reorganization of the National Health Service (NHS) in 1974, it became clear that Northville had too many maternity beds. A fall in the birthrate coupled with a move of people out of the inner city area, where Maine Road was situated, had resulted in falling bed occupancy. Apart from one particularly prestigious maternity unit, which enjoyed a very good reputation both inside and outside the city, the remaining units – Maine Road and wards at "King Street" and "Sackville" district general hospitals – were all working at about 50 per cent of their full capacity.

A plan to close Maine Road was proposed by management in 1976. Initial soundings met with the approval of the AHA and, in September, a consultative document was released, proposing the closure over the following two years, during which time the facilities at King Street and Sackville hospitals would be improved to enable them to cope with any extra demand.

Objections to these proposals were immediately expressed by a number of different groups. Staff at the hospital set up an action committee to stop the closure: they wrote to general practitioners; lobbied members of Parliament; appeared on TV and radio; spoke at a local Trades Council meeting; contacted the press; and presented the AHA with a petition of more than 10,000 signatures opposing the closure. The Community Health Council (CHC) also opposed the closure, and the National Union of Public Employees (NUPE) expressed "serious concern", arguing that the birthrate would soon rise again and the facilities at Maine Road would be needed.

Despite this furore, management pressed on with its plans. In March 1977, it issued a supplement to the consultative document, bringing forward the closure until as soon as possible after July of that year. This decision was, according to management, necessitated by the estimated deficit of £ 1 million on the annual budget. This supplemental document also mentioned, for the first time, the alternative option of closing down the wards at King Street and Sackville general hospitals and retaining Maine Road. It dismissed this option, however, because the savings would be £ 500,000 per annum less, and because of the government's policy to integrate specialist units into a general hospital, with all its back-up facilities.

The supplement caused further impetus from the opposition movement. The local media continued to report on the issue; a television program in May 1977 covered the proposed closure; there was a well-attended public meeting in May at which a consultant obstetrician at the hospital spoke against the closure. The CHC restated its opposition, proposing that maternity wards at King Street and Sackville should be closed instead. A special meeting of the AHA was called in July 1977 to consider the two options – the closure of Maine Road or the wards at Sackville and King Street. Fifteen members (out of 26) had attended, but only 9 voted – 5 to 4 in favour of the closure of Maine Road. The meeting resolved that both the AHA and the CHC should give further consideration to the two options.

The CHC continued to oppose the closure. A letter from the consultant obstetrician at Maine Road argued that the hospital should be retained because it was such a good specialist hospital. An outburst of indignation arose from the staff at Maine Road about the low turnout for the AHA meeting.

> Maine Road Action Committee members claimed there had been gross under-representation with only 11 out of a total of 26 members present at the Special Meeting. And they were angry that only eight took part in the vote (Local press article, July 1977. In fact, the numbers were incorrect: 15 attended and 9 voted.)

On the 23rd of August, another meeting of the AHA was called. Only 14 members attended, but 13 voted and the decision was 9 to 4 in favour of retaining Maine Road, and closing the wards at King Street and Sackville General hospitals instead. By July 1978, the unions had agreed to the closure of these wards; the maternity wards at Sackville closed in August 1978, and those at King Street in September.

The Reasons for Failure

Northville is a clear example of managerial failure. Management's plans were overturned by the AHA as a result of concerted opposition from a number of interest groups. Instead of closing the hospital they wanted, they were forced to close wards in other hospitals at considerable financial cost, and with serious damage to their credibility. There are three categories of reasons that help to explain this situation: previous managerial actions; the power of the opposition; and the management of the attempted closure. This section examines these factors.

Previous Managerial Actions

Since the reorganization of the National Health Service (NHS) in 1974, management had engaged in a number of actions that had earned itself distrust and suspicion, damaging its credibility in the eyes of employees, union officials, and Community Health Councils (CHC).

> To the people of Northville it seemed as though the AHA was determined to bring the local health service to its knees by a process of attrition (CHC secretary in published article, 1979).

For example, the 1974 reorganization had introduced a new administrative layer into the NHS, which had created some problems for local managers. Management had, however, exacerbated the situation by proposing a move from the two districts, established in 1974, to a single district. This change was proposed as early as 1975. Many people felt that the two district system had never been given a chance to work. Moreover, there had been an eighteen-month delay before the Secretary of State gave his consent to the change. The uncertainty caused by this delay was disastrous – morale dropped when many of the best managers fled, leaving the less experienced ones to deal with the ever increasing problems. This issue had led to considerable criticism from all parties.

> Whatever the intrinsic merits of "single district" over "two district" areas, the mistake lay in seeking so fundamental a change at a time when other problems were being faced (committee of inquiry).
>
> The fight for single district wasted time and created bitterness (manager).

> The move to single district has worsened industrial relations (steward).
>
> Perhaps the clearest illustration of the AHA's self-inflicted problem is the single district problem (CHC secretary in published article, 1979).

Another problem had been created with a decision to build a new general hospital. It had taken seventeen years and more than £50 million to build it. A lot of small community hospitals had been closed to pave the way for the "great white elephant", as it came to be called. People resented the loss of local hospitals for the much more impersonal atmosphere of such a large hospital. They were also concerned by the fact that the project had been considerably over-budget and behind schedule before the hospital was completed.

> The hospital had become a national scandal (CHC secretary in published article, 1979).
>
> The hospital is a bloody disaster. It's not the way people want to be looked after (consultant).

A third set of problems revolved around the ATO's response to financial restraints. Government spending cuts in the mid-1970s had produced general restrictions on spending. The Resource Allocation Working Party affected Northville in a similar way to Midville. In its attempt to distribute funds more fairly between health regions, it had devised a formula in August 1975, which would reduce the RHA's allocation in real terms. This budget reduction would mean the minimum increase in the following year's budget for Northville. The final recommendations were, in fact, more generous, but the 1976/1977 budget had already been distributed to the AHAs on the basis of an expected reduction in funds. Northville's situation was further exacerbated by another change in funding. Additional funds that had previously been made available for bringing new hospitals into operation were withdrawn. Since Northville AHA was just completing its new hospital, it would now have to bring it on line with money from its annual operating budget.

In response to this financial situation, the AHA had proposed drastic cuts in Northville's health services in an attempt to balance the budget.

> Inside eighteen months, two-thirds of the hospitals in the city have been or still are threatened with closure, reduction, or resignation (committee of inquiry).

Management did not, however, manage these reductions as well as it might have. There was a reluctance to share information or consult with the parties involved.

> Each time a new planning document has appeared it has been a major headline in the local press before the bulk of the staff, often including senior officers in the units concerned, were aware of its contents (committee of inquiry).
>
> Another criticism of management has been its failure to share information adequately and at the right time (committee of inquiry).

When further cuts were announced in May 1977, there was an "explosion of protest" as groups of staff, unions, and the CHCs tried to resist them. This protest was followed by union deputations to the minister, who agreed to set up a committee of inquiry; which has been quoted here, to examine management–union relations at Northville.

The Power of the Opposition

A second reason for the opposition was the power of the various opposition groups. There was a general history of militancy, radicalism, and trade unionism at Northville that did not exist, to the same extent, at Midville. For example, whereas Midville had had no local disputes since 1974 and virtually no national disputes, Northville had been beset by industrial action at both national and local levels. There had been, for example, eight disputes between October and December 1978. More than 4,000 working days had been lost in official disputes alone between January and March 1979.

The protests of union and other opposition groups were fuelled by the depressed nature of the area. Northville has a high proportion of semi-skilled, unskilled, and unemployed workers; elderly people, homeless; and single-parent families. There was an imbalance between primary and secondary health care which led to a

> strongly held view that over-bedding ... should not be tackled until there has been sufficient improvement in the quality of community care services (committee of inquiry).

This deprivation, combined with the background of militancy, led to resistance by employees and other groups against managerial decisions that threatened their services. Opposition groups were able to mobilize their power in the form of strong and supportive unions, and the network of contacts with other groups such as CHCs, tenants' associations, community groups, and political parties. They were able to solicit coverage and support from the local media.

The Management of the Closure

Finally, management failed to handle the specific issue of the Maine Road closure as well as it might have. It failed to convince anybody – the employees, the unions, the CHCs, the public, or the AHA – that the decision to close Maine Road was justified. Even though they had a commitment to the general principle of the rationalization of maternity beds, managers were unable to demonstrate medical or financial reasons for the closure.

Medical reasons were, as one would expect, a powerful influence in the health service. "It is difficult to challenge their views, as laymen" (CHC secretary). Medical reasoning is, however, difficult to evaluate. For example, the policy of large integrated hospitals calling for 1,500-bed hospitals, advocated in the 1962 Hospital Plan and the 1967 Bonham Carter Report, was reversed by the Conservative government which favoured small community hospitals (Dean, 1980). It is very difficult to judge these medical arguments objectively – the reasons that are perceived as "right" are often those which publicly receive the largest amount of medical approval. Consequently, soliciting medical support for managerial decisions is important, since doctors can legitimize an argument simply by being associated with it.

At Maine Road, the one highly visible and voluble consultant allied himself with the opposition. He emerged as a public figure and appeared in several press articles, on TV, and at the public meeting. His opinion was reinforced by other medical personnel. A new consultant on the AHA attended his first meeting on 23rd August 1977, when the vote to retain Maine Road was taken. He:

> helped to make them [the AHA members] change their minds. He made a significant remark: "If you close a hospital you can't re-open it so you are losing options, but if you close wards you can always re-open them." I feel that this influenced a lot of members when they voted (CHC secretary).

A professor of surgery, also an AHA member, was quoted in the press as saying that he was:

> worried that the staff would be unable to cope if Maine Road patients were transferred to King Street. About half the staff at Maine Road were undergraduates at the University, and if this teaching centre was closed, they would have to do practical training [outside the city] (local press article, July 1977).

Medical opinion thus appeared to be unanimous in its support for the retention of Maine Road. It made it difficult, if not impossible, for management to medically justify its proposal to close Maine Road.

> I think the situation would have been different if the medics hadn't been against closure (union official).

Managers tried to present the financial motives for the closure, arguing that the closure would save an estimated £500,000 per annum more than the alternative. These financial arguments were not, however, accepted. It is doubtful whether, in Northville, financial criteria constituted legitimate justification for the reduction of services. The 1977 protest against cutbacks had been organized despite the fact that financial restrictions had been forced on management. The high unemployment, urban decline, poverty, and inadequate primary care in Northville seemed to rule out service cuts on the basis of finance alone.

> NUPE [our union] is always opposed to closures on financial grounds – they probably put too much weight on finance (NUPE official).

The inability to use either medical or financial arguments to justify the closure meant that management was unable to legitimize its plans in the eyes of the employees, the unions, the CHCs, the public which campaigned against the closure, or the AHA which voted for retention.

> There has got to be a very well-argued case for closure, people need convincing. They are going to have to be satisfied that the reasons for the closure are credible (manager).

Management also failed to anticipate the emotional appeal of the hospital. It was the largest maternity hospital in the U.K., many local people had either been born there or had had their babies there; it had survived the Blitz during World War Two; and its output consisted of appealing newborn babies. Such factors may not have carried much weight with managers, but they undoubtedly attracted the public which supported the action committee in its fight against the closure. As a result, the media picked up the story. The emotive appeal of the hospital was enough to legitimize the case for retention in the eyes of the public. Management also neglected to use an opportunity for dividing public opinion. They did not make it clear that, if Maine Road did not close, the maternity wards at the other two hospitals would. Had they done so, they could have weakened public support for Maine Road. As it was, many people supported Maine Road without fully appreciating the consequences; had they known the outcome, some interviewees indicated they would have acted differently.

Public opinion was particularly important in Northville because of the local councillors, who made up one-third of the AHA membership. They were voted into office as councillors and were, therefore, sensitive to public opinion. It was particularly true of Northville because there was no clear-cut majority in the local government – the balance of power fluctuated between all three major parties. As a result, local councillors were keen to champion any cause that would win them votes. Maine Road appears to have been such a cause – the proposal to retain Maine Road was proposed and seconded by councillors. There were, however, only five councillors present at the August meeting. Since the vote was 9:4 in favour of retention (exact details of voting are not recorded), it indicates that other AHA members, persuaded by either public or medical opinion, were also in favour of retention.

Summary and Conclusions

The attempt to close Maine Road failed. It can be attributed partly to a well-orchestrated opposition campaign organized by powerful union, employee, and committee groups. Part of the blame must lie with management by virtue of its past actions, as well as its handling of this specific issue. It was unprepared for opposition and, as a result, unable to close the hospital even though many groups agreed with the need for the rationalization of maternity services in the city.

> Management misread the situation. They had an incontrovertible case for rationalization. They should have done better market research (union official).

This situation contrasts sharply with Midville, where managers had identified potential opposition groups, were well prepared to deal with them and, thus, able to provide acceptable reasons for the closure. Northville, on the other hand, ignored or failed to recognize stakeholders even though they clearly existed.

Northville managers should have been more aware that these various groups had the power to challenge their decisions. The activism of the unions and the CHCs was clearly apparent. Moreover, May 1977 had brought about the committee of inquiry into industrial relations at Northville – as a result of union protest. Having identified the groups, managers should then have been better prepared to deal with them – engaging in more consultation, sharing information, negotiating with them, and presenting a clear case why the closure was necessary.

> We were pretty naive in terms of public relations ... we were pretty naive in terms of industrial relations ... we hadn't the skill to negotiate with all these different interest groups (manager).

It is difficult to say what would have happened had the AHA voted to proceed with the closure. The CHC would probably have registered a formal protest, sending the final decision up to the minister. Union members suggested that they would have organized an occupation if there had been no reprieve. Such a threat might have motivated the minister to revoke the closure, particularly since the recent protest had already brought about the committee in inquiry. Nevertheless, management could have improved its chances of success. They could have weakened the opposition by justifying the need for closure and dealing more effectively with public sentiment. Such actions would have made the AHA more receptive to the idea of closure and, had the decision been passed upwards, would have improved the chances of ministerial approval.

Both economic and political problems continued to plague Northville during the 1980s, when a £7 million reduction in funding had to be absorbed. Deficits of £1.7 million and £1.6 million were recorded in 1982 and 1983, and spending was cut by £15 million between 1982 and 1985. More recently, administrators have been pointing to superior economic performance as a surplus of £9 million was recorded in 1984. Their critics, however, have argued that it has been at a cost of a net loss of 200 beds in 1984 alone, with an expected loss of another 700 beds and 800 full-time-equivalent posts, as well as longer waiting lists.

Summary: Ignoring Political Pressures

The organizations discussed up until Northville placed the political component of retrenchment high on their list of priorities. Even Ville Marie, which initially appeared to emphasize external politics – negotiating with the government – at the expense of internal politics – consulting and involving employees and union representatives, eventually took the steps necessary to resolve conflict. Northville, in contrast, totally and inappropriately neglected the political requirements of cutbacks. The discussion of Midville has already illustrated that hospital closure in the NHS is an intensely political process. Ignoring these political pressures, as Northville did, is a recipe for failure, as the outcome clearly shows.

Northville was surrounded by various stakeholders with sufficient power to disrupt its plans. The same groups existed at Midville – unions, CHCs, public, politicians, AHA, local councillors – but, if anything, they represented a greater threat at Northville. Part of the reason lay with previous managerial actions, which had alienated these groups to such an extent that they were highly motivated to intervene. Midville managers, in contrast, had adopted a far more consultative approach to industrial relations prior to the closure.

Midville managers, having identified their potential opponents, developed specific strategies to deal with them. So, for example, the unions and CHC were neutralized by consultation; the staff by choices between redundancy or new jobs; the doctors by new wards; and the public by open information sharing. The AHA's support was secured by a presentation of the financial situation; and the possibility of a reversal by the Department of Health and Social Security was reduced by neutralizing opposition groups. Northville managers, on the other hand, alienated most of their stakeholders. They were unable to demonstrate medical reasons for the closure; they ineptly tried to use illegitimate financial criteria; they failed to use the media; they did nothing to counteract public support for Maine Road; and they failed to convince the decisions makers – the AHA – of the validity of their plans. Consequently, the opposition to the closure was widespread, and involved staff, doctors, the CHC, the union, the public, and the AHA. This combined resistance led to a vote to retain the hospital, against management's recommendations and at a cost of £ 500,000 a year, at a time of severe financial problems.

Northville managers apparently placed much greater emphasis on economic issues: the budget deficit had provoked a flurry of cutback activity in which two-thirds of the hospitals in the city had been threatened with closure, reduction, or redesignation. Managing the numerous interest groups with the capacity to intervene in and block the closure received much less consideration. Ironically, it was this lack of attention that provoked the opposition which, ultimately, prevented managers from realizing their plans and making the required cost savings. In effect, Northville incorrectly dismissed the importance of political pressures.

This section on the organizations shows how economic and political pressures interact in the case of retrenchment to provide a network of often conflicting constraints, which managers must accommodate if they are to be successful. Retrenchment, by definition, involves economic problems but, particularly in cases where it is linked to turnaround, it also incorporates a political component. This political aspect has been defined in terms of managing the various interest groups which have the power to intervene in managerial decision making. Eight of the nine organizations discussed here voluntarily and consciously accepted the political reality of their task. Three had sufficient flexibility to be able to devote their attention to managing the political component. Five organizations were more constrained by economic considerations, and faced the delicate task of balancing them with political concerns. One organization mistakenly ignored political realities and, as a result, failed to carry out its plans. The remainder of the book focusses more explicitly on the lessons that can be learnt from the experiences of these organizations.

Part II: The Lessons

Introduction

The following chapters use the experiences of the case studies to provide some lessons in the management of retrenchment. They examine how different retrenchment strategies can be formulated to accommodate the particular situation of the organization; and how those strategies can be effectively implemented. Resistance to retrenchment is examined to illustrate the political nature of cutbacks. This political analysis is used to develop a broader framework for managers faced with resistance and conflict in other situations.

In effect, this second part of the book attempts to draw some conclusions as to why the organizations adopted the strategies that they did. It concludes that managers' perceptions of their political and economic environments explain strategic choice. A model is then derived from these findings, which shows how environments might be more accurately assessed in order to help managers find the appropriate strategy to meet their needs. In other words, this part of the book moves from the *description* of how strategies were selected based on perceptions, which were not always accurate, to *prescriptions* about how strategies should be selected to meet the objective pressures of a particular retrenchment. Finally, this model is extended to provide a broader framework for managers, who have to assess political constraints in situations other than retrenchment.

Chapter 11: Choosing a Retrenchment Strategy

The first chapter discussed the competing political and economic demands that often affect retrenchment. The following chapter illustrated how a variety of organizations attempted to balance those demands. The framework described in chapter 1 was applied to their experiences to show how a retrenchment strategy was selected to meet the perceived requirements of the situation (*diagram 4*). All the successful organizations were aware that the political dimension of retrenchment was a crucial factor in both the successful implementation of the cutbacks, and the longer-term survival of the company. Some were able to focus on managing the interest groups, while others had to balance it with economic constraints. The least successful case study

Diagram 4: Economic and Political Pressures: The Issues

		Economic Pressures	
		Unimportant	Important
Political Pressures	Important	*Managing the Interest Groups* ICI CIL Whitefields	*Balancing Economic and Political Pressures* Andersons Midville AECL Air Canada Ville Marie
	Unimportant	*Free of Pressures*	*Ignoring Political Pressures* Northville

– Northville – illustrates the dangers of inaccurately undervaluing the importance of political realities.

Choosing Effective Strategies

The organizations developed a variety of different strategies to help them meet the requirements of their situation as they saw it. We can generalize from these case studies to provide a general framework for choosing retrenchment strategies. In other words, an analysis of how managers perceived political and economic pressures helps to explain why they acted the way they did. We can move beyond this descriptive approach, by showing how an accurate appraisal of the environment should influence strategic choice. This chapter elaborates on how managers can choose appropriate strategies for retrenchment and turnaround.

There are certain key assumptions that underlie the framework presented in this chapter. First, retrenchment is considered to be a part of a turnaround strategy. The book is concerned with organizations that are cutting back in order to protect the whole. Previous work on business turnaround (for example, Hambrick & Schecter, 1983; Hofer, 1980; Schendel & Patton, 1976; Schendel et al., 1976) has argued that it is important to match the type of turnaround to the cause of decline. If the underlying cause is a structural shift in markets, the response should be strategic turnaround, which involves changing the product/market mix. If decline relates to internal inefficiency, the organization should seek ways of increasing revenue, cutting costs, and decreasing assets, i.e., engage in operating turnaround. The retrenchment strategies described here are consistent with both turnaround strategies: factories may be closed to cut overheads, or as the result of phasing out of certain products; hospitals may be shut to reduce costs or to reorient services.

This business literature views turnaround primarily as an economic problem when it is, in fact, also a political problem (Hardy, 1987a). The second assumption, then, is that turnaround has a political dimension – because of the various interest groups that have a stake in the rundown and recovery process. The most important group is often the employees. Turnaround will depend on the ability to maintain high levels of morale, motivation (Bilbeault, 1982), and commitment, which is particularly important when scarce resources escalate levels of political conflict. Employees often possess the power to resist cutbacks through their unions; and continuing employees are central to successful turnaround. Consequently, engaging in a retrenchment program that caters specifically to the needs of employees is often one means of accommodating these political pressures. There are other groups that may also play important roles, for example, the media, politicians, and other relevant interests.

It would appear, clearly, then, that retrenchment decisions involve two often conflicting pressures. One emanating from short-term economic demands, and the other from the needs of employees and other stakeholders (Hardy, 1986 a). The economic dimension requires both the efficient allocation of internal resources and effective external strategies (Wamsley & Zald, 1973), corresponding to the operational and strategic turnaround strategies discussed by Hofer (1980). The political dimension involves mobilizing commitment to recovery and the containment of any conflict between potential opponents. The political component of retrenchment and turnaround is thus defined as the management of commitment and conflict (see Wamsley & Zald, 1973). This juxtaposition of economic and political pressures in decision making is not new (see, for example, Astley et al., 1982; Wamsley & Zald, 1973). The question is, however, how it should be managed in the context of retrenchment. The following *diagram 5* illustrates some of the appropriate strategies.

Managing the Interest Groups

In this situation, managers feel that managing the different interest groups is crucial to successful retrenchment and turnaround. Moreover, the organization has sufficient resources in the way of time and money to allow managers to mitigate economic pressures and focus on the political side of retrenchment. Their aim is to reassure the different groups that their interests are being accommodated and the cutbacks are being managed in a responsible way.

The organization, since it has time on its side, should consider alternative methods of retrenchment such as attrition, early retirement, and

Diagram 5: Economic and Political Pressures: The Strategies

		Economic Pressures	
		Unimportant	Important
Political Pressures	Important	*Managing the Interest Groups* -alternative methods -voluntary dismissals -support measures [1]	*Balancing Economic and Political Pressures* -voluntary dismissals with conditions -enforced dismissals with support measures [2]
	Unimportant	[4] *Free of Pressures* -free choice	[3] *Ignoring Politics* -enforced dismissals -no support

worksharing. Attrition is one of the least painful ways of reducing personnel and should be one of the first responses to the need for cuts (Ellig, 1983; Hammerman, 1964; Hercus, 1978). However, since it is a relatively slow process, its use is confined to those organizations which have sufficient time to allow for the reduction of personnel in this way. Early retirement is a way to speed up attrition, and it has the advantage of not being perceived as a redundancy program (Ellig, 1983; Gravitz, 1983; Hammerman, 1964; Hercus, 1978). It provides an opportunity to free promotion channels and allow young employees into the organization. It can also be used to offset the effects of layoffs, by enabling older employees to vacate jobs for younger personnel.

Worksharing has attracted a lot of attention (see, for example, Benson, 1982; Blyton, 1982; Eleen & Ashley, 1971; Hercus, 1978; McNeff et al., 1978; Meltz et al., 1981; Sadlier-Brown, 1978). It reduces the need for layoffs, enables skilled employees to remain with the organization, and maintains a workforce should demand improve. Productivity may increase through reduced absenteeism and increased flexibility and commitment. For some industries, however, worksharing is impractical. There may also be a lack of union interest. Worksharing involves increased costs to the firm of 0.5–1 per cent of the gross payroll for employment insurance, pension plans, and health insurance.

If redundancies become necessary, the company can afford voluntary severance. Voluntary dismissals have considerable political benefits in that only those workers who so choose leave the organization. Those remaining will view a voluntary program much more favourably – perceiving the terminations to be a matter of choice rather than an arbitrary decision by the firm, which will help to protect morale and commitment.

Support measures can be used to offset the impact of redundancy. Advance notice[1] is a support mechanism which has stirred up considerable controversy. Employers have objected on the grounds that productivity and morale fall, and it results in people leaving before final production requirements have been met. Most of these problems do not appear to materialize, however. People do not leave early on any significant scale, which is hardly surprising since most layoffs are linked to adverse economic conditions that make other jobs difficult to find; and to severance benefits, which are tied to specific termination dates. Employees derive considerable benefit from advance notice. It increases their chances of finding new jobs. It allows layoffs to be staggered, and provides time for the organization of outplacement aid and retraining. It acts as a cushion for the shock of displacement, and gives the community a chance to adjust, which may be particularly important in the event of a plant closure in an isolated or depressed area (see Batt, 1983, Carrothers et al., 1979; Eleen & Ashley, 1971; Gordus et al., 1981; Morin & Yorks, 1982; Portis & Suys, 1970; Sexton, 1974; Shultz & Weber, 1966; Stern, 1967; Ullman, 1969; Weber & Taylor, 1963).

Consultation and communication help to dispel the rumours and myths that inevitably accompany layoffs, and demonstrate that the

[1] In Britain, 3 months advance notice is required for more than 100 redundancies. The Canada Labour Code requires organizations to provide 16 weeks notice (Carrothers et al., 1979). Notice is also required in some provinces (Harrison, 1984; Sexton, 1974). Most US states have negligible legislation regarding advance notice, although some unions have negotiated it into their contracts (Batt, 1983; Labour Relations Yearbook, 1980).

company is trying to be honest with its employees (Greenhalgh, 1983; Stybel, 1978; Sutton, 1983). Consultation between management and employees can be a useful way to address such problems as outplacement and grievances, thereby creating trust and understanding, as well as finding concrete solutions. Employers have argued against joint consultation on the grounds that the decision for layoffs is a managerial one (for example, Whyte, 1982). Others acknowledge the value of the unions's contribution to that process once the decision has been made (Carrothers et al., 1979).

Outplacement aid helps employees to find new jobs. There are a number of ways in which it can be achieved (see, for example, Foltman, 1968; Fuller et al., 1982; Hammerman, 1964; Hercus, 1978; Levine, 1983; Portis & Suys, 1970; Stern, 1969; Ullman, 1969). Such services are not costly, and are important for two reasons. They provide very real help to individuals in their search for new employment; and they are of great symbolic value. They signal that the company does care about its employees and is prepared to carry out certain responsibilities, even towards those who are leaving. It helps to allay the fears and insecurities of continuing employees.

Retraining is a more complex way of helping the employee find a new job, requiring more commitment and money on the part of the company (see, for example, Burke et al., 1983; Hammerman, 1964; Monthly Labour Review, 1961). The employer pays for the cost of retraining, which may be done by a professional agency, a government department, or in-house. The travel costs and living expenses of the individual during retraining may also be paid. Internal transfers reduce job losses through the redeployment of workers to other parts of the company. Relocation expenses are usually provided, and additional financial assistance may be available. Employees may be offered a free trip to evaluate the new location.

Severance pay is compulsory in Britain[2], although only minimal provisions exist in North America. It helps compensate individuals who

---

[2] Employers must pay 1/2 week's pay per year of service to employees aged 18–21, 1 week's pay to employees aged 22–40, and 1 1/2 week's pay to employees aged 41–65. Employees must have 2 years' service to qualify and can receive up to a maximum of 20 years' service. The state reimburses 41% of this amount from a fund set up in 1965.

have lost their jobs, providing a cushion while they are looking for a new job. Severance pay is important not only in the financial assistance it provides, but also in demonstrating that the company places a value on its employees and cares for their wellbeing (Luce, 1983).

Balancing Economic and Political Pressures

In this situation, the organization has to weigh the need to make quick and effective cuts against the need to protect employee morale or accommodate other stakeholders. Economic constraints might, for example, mean that the organization has insufficient time to adopt alternative methods of downsizing, and layoffs may be inevitable. Managers might be worried about the loss of critical skills and, so, be reluctant to adopt voluntary severance. Enforced dismissals may also be deemed necessary if, for example, voluntary measures will not make the necessary cost savings quickly enough, or if the organization is unable to provide lucrative incentives.

Organizations in this position may be able to adopt voluntary severance, but retain their control by imposing conditions that prevent the loss of key skills or experience. Enforced dismissals are also a likely strategy. They are cheaper than voluntary severance since no incentives are necessary. They also afford more control over who is terminated, allowing skills and performance to be protected or specific departments to be phased out. If selective dismissals are employed, some form of support will be necessary to help those employees faced with job loss and to reassure continuing employees. Of particular importance will be outplacement services to help terminated employees find new jobs. It is possible to provide significant aid at a relatively low cost. Employers can write to or telephone other organizations, particularly where they have contacts, to see if they are interested in hiring the displaced workers. They can advertize to the same effect or ask employers to notify them of any vacancies. By providing skill inventories of their employees, they are in a position to match people to job offers. Individuals can be counselled in how to go about job searching, and rehearsed in writing resumes, filling out application forms, and attending interviews. Typing and other services can be provided.

Ignoring Political Pressures

Some organizations may feel that economic constraints take precedence over political concerns. If it is an accurate assessment of the situation, managers can choose those actions that ensure rapid cutbacks at minimum cost. Likely strategies are selected/enforced dismissals and little in the way of support mechanisms. Managers are unlikely to provide much aid to employees or to engage in any dialogue with other interest groups. Minimum standards dictated by law may be the only protection for employees.

It is important, however, to stress that such strategies are only appropriate if managers have made an *accurate* assessment of their situation. If they have mistakenly overlooked interest groups that can adversely influence their plans; if they have underestimated the importance of employee and union commitment to the long-term survival of the organization; if they have *mistakenly* categorized their situation, ignoring political pressures will only lead to failure, as the example of Northville clearly shows.

Free of Pressures

It is rare that employers will be free of both political and economic constraints. Asset stripping might be considered to be one example. In this situation, employers are, theoretically, free to choose the retrenchment program they desire.

Summary and Conclusions

This chapter has used the experiences of the case studies to formulate a framework that helps managers to choose retrenchment strategies that meet the needs of their particular situation. Both political and economic demands can be accommodated with the careful selection of a strategy. A long-term perspective, which links retrenchment and turnaround, has been presented. It stresses that successful turnaround owes as much to managing politics as economics. For this reason, the focus has been on the first two categories of the framework, where politics is an important ingredient of success. The framework recognizes that some organizations may be faced with pressing economic constraints, in which case they must find the appropriate strategy to deal with declining markets, revenues, and profits. These strategies are relatively well served by the existing literature on turnaround, and it is not, therefore, the intention of this book to elaborate on them; rather, it is to emphasize the political dimension, which has received far less coverage.

It is also important to stress that apparent recommendations for an economic focus should be treated with caution by managers, for two reasons. First, while these oganizations may have economic concerns, they should not abrogate their ethical responsibility to their employees. In some countries, such as the USA, protective legislation is minimal, and organizations can do a lot to soften the blow of cutbacks. So, there may be a moral duty on the part of organizations to provide their employees with more than the basic minimum. Second, because of the preoccupation with retrenchment as an economic phenomenon, managers run a great risk of focussing on the short term and the economic, while ignoring the longer-term issues and the political component of retrenchment. In other words, the mistake that managers would seem most likely to make in assessing their situation would appear to be that of adopting the third position, instead of the second. As the case of Northville clearly shows – ignoring political factors when they do, in fact, exist will almost inevitably lead to failure.

The framework is based on the experiences of both U.K. and Canadian organizations, which raises the issue of cultural differences. The two major differences between the two countries appear to be the following. The U.K. has a much stronger history of overt resistance to retrenchment, as will be discussed in the next chapter. There are also differences in legislation which mean that, for the most part, British workers are relatively better protected than their Canadian counterparts. These differences notwithstanding, the strategic framework is applicable to both countries. The lack of overt resistance does not remove the political component of retrenchment. Union resistance can take other forms, and other stakeholders still exist. Moreover, the need to sustain commitment and motivation among continuing employees for turnaround is equally applicable to both countries. Nor do the differences in legislation preclude organizations from using voluntary severance and the various support measures; although they may have to tailor them to their own specific needs, and use the infrastructure that exists.

This chapter has, then, provided a framework for choosing an appropriate retrenchment strategy. It is one thing, however, to formulate a strategy; it is another to see it implemented particularly in the contentious atmosphere of retrenchment. The following chapter discusses some of the ways in which these strategies can be put into action.

Chapter 12: Putting the Strategies into Action

Retrenchment is a highly contentious issue. Even if the retrenchment strategy has been formulated with the needs of the various interest groups in mind, resources are still being reduced. As a result, many people stand to lose from the implementation of a retrenchment strategy – their jobs, their position, their status. Consequently, they may take steps to block cutbacks by mobilizing the power sources they have at their disposal. It is this political dimension of retrenchment that makes its implementation a difficult task. The problem is compounded by the fact that many organizations are still geared up for growth; and managers may be unwilling to acknowledge decline, much less discuss the best ways of handling it. This chapter discusses some of the steps that can be taken to ease the process of implementation. It also examines the critical role of the human resource manager in putting retrenchment strategies into action.

Steps Towards Implementation

There are a number of tasks that can be carried out to reduce the chances of resistance to retrenchment strategies and enhance the likelihood of successful retrenchment (Hardy, 1987 a). Also see, for example, Gordus et al., 1981; Greenhalgh, 1983; Luce, 1983; Sutton, 1983, 1986.

Managing Awareness

Awareness of the importance of social and political implications of retrenchment as a part of the larger turnaround strategy must be created among the senior level of management, for two reasons: to ensure that the necessary cuts are made in a timely and logical manner, avoiding a crisis and allowing for a more humane approach to be put into place; and to secure a commitment among decision makers to a more enlightened approach and the investment which it entails. Working groups were established at ICI in 1975 to establish the exact nature of individual needs, key personnel and communication and retraining requirements during the rundown process. CIL established a planning committee well before the announcement of the closure to work out the specific details.

A lack of awareness of the need for downsizing will result in counterproductive decisions which aggravate an already difficult situation. AECL's hiring of graduates only to lay them off is an example. It not only compromised managers' credibility, it left them with the difficulties of laying off additional staff, and dealing with a disaffected group of people who had turned down other jobs to work for AECL. Potential recruits may well look a little more critically at AECL's hiring promises in the future.

Difficulties in predicting the future with any degree of certainty can be overcome. Managers at Ville Marie did not know by how much the government planned to cut their budget, so they worked out three cutback scenarios. The knowledge accumulated in this process put them in a good position to effect the 11 per cent cut they ultimately received.

Senior managers will provide the funds necessary to protect and support employees only if they consider it to be a worthwhile investment. Divisional and human resource managers at CIL presented the executive committee with nine reasons why they should handle the closure carefully, ranging from the possibility of sabotage and other potential union problems to the difficulties of finding alternative employment in such an isolated area. The result was that the retrenchment program was approved, as were the funds required to carry it out.

Managing the Alternatives

The aim of creating awareness is to buy time and commitment. This allows a more flexible approach to downsizing, including the opportunity to consider some of the alternative methods of reducing costs. If action is taken early enough, attrition can be used to reduce personnel. Worksharing, early retirement, and voluntary severance as well as leaves of absence, pay freezes, and redeployments to other locations are other options for cost cutting.

These alternative methods involve an additional cost to the employer and may take longer to have an effect. Employers, therefore, need to be well prepared to be able to make use of them. Creating awareness and planning ahead helps an organization to reduce the short-term economic restraints and spend more attention on accommodating employees. In this way, ICI used its five-year lead time to enable attrition to reduce the need for redundancies, which enabled it to have a voluntary program.

Criticisms that voluntary programs are too expensive do not appear to be valid. Even at AECL where more than 500 had already been laid off at the height of the recession, and where the incentive "was not a rich package", 80 people took advantage of it. The concern that the best people would leave was not borne out in the experiences of the organizations, since people had loyalties which bound them to the organization "regardless of the job market". Managers felt it was often the marginal performers who left: perhaps because they were disillusioned with their jobs, and voluntary severance provided an opportunity to leave; perhaps because they feared a less honourable discharge later. Even when experience was lost, the opening up of promotion opportunities for younger staff more than compensated, as at Air Canada.

The company can always protect itself by stating formal conditions. Air Canada reserved the right of refusal in cases where scarce skills would be lost to the competition. Informal persuasion can be used to ease out some of the more marginal performers. However, voluntary programs must be *seen* to be voluntary to be effective. Managers must not be viewed as "leaning" on people. Nor must there be too many denials: even at Air Canada there was pressure from the CEO down to let everyone go unless there were some "really dire circumstances". It also means accepting the numbers who apply, be they above or below expectations. Managers at Whitefields were willing to cut expenses or to carry the extra overhead rather than fire anyone in the event that an insufficient number of people volunteered.

Voluntary severance provides both the company and the employee with benefits. Employees are given a choice, and there is no stigma attached to their dismissal. The company gains credibility by being seen to accommodate employee needs, which translates into commitment and productivity from continuing employees.

Managing Involvement

Employees will be worried about the impact the cutbacks will have on them. Involving representatives in at least part of the decision-making process helps to reduce feelings of powerlessness, and provides a forum in which employee interests can be protected.

Companies that restricted involvement met with criticism. Andersons refused to allow union participation in the feasibility study, or to release the figures on which the recommendation for closure was based. The result was a great deal of suspicion concerning the company's motives and an unwillingness to believe that the closure was necessary.

> Andersons has a traditional position – they make a decision and the union agrees ... I think they made a mistake. If they'd come to the same decision with union involvement, it would have been easier to accept (union official).

Beliefs that effective involvement cannot be created around the issue of cutbacks are unfounded. Mechanisms were established to facilitate employee involvement in most of the organizations. At Mountside a special committee was set up with union and management representation to secure the cooperation of the senior stewards. It brought together the two sides as a problem-solving group, avoiding the need to resort to the formal negotiating procedure. It made recommendations concerning employee needs to the works manager, who was then able to take decisions fully aware of the likely consequences. He sometimes made concessions (for example, allowing people to leave before their termination date with full severance pay if they had found another job), which helped win the goodwill of the stewards. They felt they were an active part of the process, able to safeguard their members' interests rather than having to watch helplessly from the sidelines. This committee thus acted as a safety valve, achieving a "remarkable degree of trust on both sides", and preventing any industrial unrest.

Placement committees were established with managers and union representatives at CIL to consider the issues of retraining, counselling, and outplacement. Federal legislation dictated the establishment of a Joint Planning Committee at AECL, but the corporation also set up other committees for each of the four employee groups to handle grievances and outplacement needs.

Managing Fair Play

Employees were reassured by a sense of fair play in how the process was handled, particularly when managers were forced to undertake dismissals involving some sort of selection process. A perception of fairness prevents the initiation of grievances and provides some security to continuing employees.

Three common selection criteria are seniority, required skills, and performance. Seniority has the advantage of being a criterion that workers "relate to", helping them to view dismissals "in a rational fashion" and to accept the choices that are made. Some critics argue that it robs the organization of its younger recruits. The problem with the alternative criteria is that they are more subjective, and decisions may be contested. Unions at AECL disagreed with the selection criteria that were used to protect critical skills and initiated over 100 grievances.

On another issue, AECL's sense of fair play was commended: its willingness to handle unionized and non-unionized groups in the same way. Of the four employee groups at the corporation, only two were represented by unions. However, committees were set up on the same basis for all these groups, and management established grievance procedures for the non-unionized employees who were not protected by collective agreements.

Discrimination between management and non-management employees also creates a sense of injustice. Air Canada ran into this problem: voluntary severance was offered only to managers on the basis that their jobs were being terminated permanently. Other employees were laid off on a temporary basis according to union contracts and did not qualify for the same severance pay. Despite the difference in the nature of the layoffs, union representatives felt that their members were being discriminated against, and management had a difficult time explaining its position to them.

Managing Support

It was argued in the previous chapter that managers can accommodate interest group concerns by choosing a strategy that includes support measures. They can prove invaluable in helping employees deal with job loss, enhancing managerial credibility in the eyes of both departing and continuing employees, and providing a firm foundation for future employee relations. Of particular importance here are attempts to reduce the insecurity of employees, such as severance pay and help in finding new jobs.

All the firms provided some sort of redundancy compensation or severance pay, and many provided outplacement aid. Andersons and ICI exceeded the legal minimum. Air Canada offered up to eighteen months' pay. Whitefields offered two years' salary over the following four years. CIL instituted a minimum of $4,000 and paid between one and two weeks' pay per year of service. AECL offered one week's pay per year of service with a variety of supplements providing up to an additional fifty-five days' pay for some employees.

In terms of outplacement aid, ICI advertized on behalf of its employees, appointed a redeployment manager, set up a "job shop" in which vacancies were posted, provided training in interview skills, and allowed paid time off to attend interviews. CIL provided job search seminars, moving expenses, job search expenses, paid time off, retirement counselling, and financial planning. AECL undertook "ad tracking" on behalf of employees, posted vacancies, advertized, provided seminars on job search techniques, offered secretarial support, staffed an outplacement centre, and organized a job fair in which potential employers were invited on site. This type of aid has a positive impact at a relatively low cost.

> There's no denying that providing that sort of [outplacement] aid helps the acceptance of the pain of workforce reduction. ... It really doesn't cost you that much. It costs a lot in time and effort in the organizing, but it doesn't cost you in terms of dollars in cash outlay, and in some respects it's more appreciated (manager).

Managers at Andersons took a somewhat different approach. First, they tried to save some jobs by transferring a substitute product to the Scottish factory. When it failed, they hired a consultant to conduct an international search for a buyer for the factory and equipment. While it proved unsuccessful, a local search, instigated by the company and its employees, uncovered a demand for the engineering skills of the workforce. As a result, a small subcontracting engineering firm was set up with the company's help, employing about 200 of the original employees.

Managing Disclosure

Empirical studies agree that it is in the employees' interests if managers disclose as much information as they can, as soon as they can, as often as they can. Advance notice improves morale and enhances the chances of finding another job. The absence of information, on the other hand, leads to rumour which is usually more pessimistic than reality. Some managers at Ville Marie withheld information, believing it would add to anxiety to say too much about impending cuts. Employees, however, found that the resulting rumours increased uncertainty and tension.

CIL sent specially trained counsellors to the closing plant on the day of the announcement "to get as much information to all the employees as quickly as possible". Even though they were not legally required to do so, AECL managers informed individuals of their future at the same time as the announcement of group dismissals, to avoid the entire corporation worrying about job losses and having a detrimental effect on production.

Advance notice does not necessarily result in conflict, sabotage, or declining productivity, as is sometimes charged. The percentage of hours lost due to industrial action fell at Andersons from 18 per cent in 1977 to less than 1 per cent in the first nine months of 1979, after the announcement of redundancies. Absenteeism fell during the rundown process at Mountside, as did the number of customer complaints, while the output per man-week remained stable. Productivity actually rose at CIL.

It is not enough simply to inform employees at the beginning of the exercise: information should be updated as the retrenchment program progresses. A weekly bulletin at Mountside was issued in both a newsheet and via the internal telephone. It ran for more than two years and was revised weekly to ensure that employees were aware of what was happening.

Information should be realistic – raising false hopes can backfire. At Brookside, three statements indicating that there was no threat to jobs were made shortly before the closure was announced. The actual announcement took employees by surprise, and they started to question the company's motives, blaming the closure on ineffective planning, and accusing it of hiding the real situation from them.

Managing Understanding

From the effective disclosure of information should come an understanding of why retrenchment is occurring, which is important if union officials and employees are to accept the cuts. Understanding stems from demonstrating legitimate reasons for retrenchment. Opposition arose at Northville because medical reasons for the cuts were disputed by medical staff, while the financial rationale was considered an unacceptable basis on which to cut health services.

Air Canada took a number of steps to create an understanding of the corporation's position throughout the organization. An audiovisual program was created called "The Air Canada Challenge", involving a film, articles in the company magazine, and meetings between managers and employees. It was used to explain what was happening in the industry in terms of costs, declining markets, and deregulation. Individuals were informed of the steps being taken to deal with these problems – the marketing efforts to attract new business, the measures to save gasoline, the steps to increase efficiency. Finally, it impressed upon employees the need for sacrifices, cost cutting, and increased productivity.

Managing Blame

One issue that will arise from trying to create an understanding of the reasons behind the cutbacks is the question of who is to blame for them. Managers have to choose between accepting responsibility for the current situation and directing the blame elsewhere. The latter can be a very risky strategy: if employees find out that the reasons for cutbacks are not valid, they will start to question the entire retrenchment exercise, and management will find itself the subject of a great deal of suspicion.

Anderson's attempt to blame the closure on falling world demand was contested by the unions who felt it was a "cosmetic exercise" designed to placate financial institutions worried about their investments. The closure was interpreted as a political move rather than a financial necessity, and the unions felt that they could pressure the company into changing its decision.

Managers can sometimes take advantage of an external scapegoat. Although the Mountside closure was part of a rationalization plan, managers tended to blame it on the old age of the plant, and the proximity of the potentially dangerous chemical plant to a hospital and residential area. These reasons were visible, comprehensible, and had the added advantage of absolving management from all blame. In this case the "scapegoating" worked. As did a similar situation at Midville AHA where a proposed hospital closure was blamed on government spending cuts, even though the planned concentration of services in the general hospital would have led to the closure in any event. If a clearly visible scapegoat exists, which does not implicate management and which is easy to understand, managers may choose to use it. If, however, the explanation is complicated or contentious, this strategy may well backfire.

These steps described above can smooth the implementation process and help increase the chances of success. Much of the work in this area will become the responsibility of the human resource manager. The next section looks at this role more closely.

The Role of the Human Resource Manager

It has repeatedly been stressed that retrenchment is only the first step of a turnaround strategy. For retrenchment to play its part in the revitalization of the organization, it has to be part of an integrated strategy to restore competitiveness; with a focus on *all* the necessary ingredients for success. The problem is that senior managers may define cutbacks as a purely economic phenomenon and, as a result, the steps above will be ignored. It may fall to the human resource manager to convince line management and key policy makers of the need to accommodate employees, unions, and other interest groups. It may be a difficult task. Retrenchment is usually necessitated by adverse environmental conditions which have brought about considerable uncertainty, if not panic. The organization may be in turmoil with crisis decision making prevailing over a broader, long-term perspective. Line managers will be preoccupied with the need to save money, meet budgets, reduce overheads, and raise productivity. Employee concerns may be pushed down the list of priorities.

> Some [line] managers won't do anything if they can't see a buck in it, and in tight business conditions they have more power (human resource manager).

Human resource managers face a number of challenges if they are to prevent decisions being taken purely on the basis of cost criteria, and human resource personnel being brought in solely to "pick up the pieces" (Hardy, 1986b). They are responsible for the protection of human resources (both those leaving and those staying) in order to help the organization restore viability. They may have to change the climate if it is unsupportive of the measures necessary to protect these employees. They must try to ensure that human resource management plays an integral role in strategy making and policy making for the organization. Managing these issues successfully will enable human resource managers to carry out their jobs more effectively and, in so doing, to produce benefits for the employees, the organization, and the human resource function itself.

Human resource managers are often limited to an administrative role, as personnel managers are charged with implementing the mechanics of the policy decisions taken at executive levels. This aspect of retrenchment is not unimportant – organizing outplacement aid, severance pay, and pension and other benefits is a complex process requiring considerable time, energy, and expertise. Human resource managers can, however, play a much more central role in preparing the organization for retrenchment.

At ICI the works manager – appointed for his "people orientation" – started to initiate a culture change four years before the closure was announced, believing that it was crucial to the success of the closure. The foundations of the consultative machinery were in place before the issue of closure arose; working relationships and a considerable amount of trust between management and the stewards had already been built up. A similar situation arose at CIL where another people-oriented individual was appointed before the announcement of the partial closure. He, too, believed that the three years, during which he changed union attitudes towards the company, were instrumental in producing such a smooth exercise. Midville managers had been consolidating industrial relations since the 1974 reorganization, and felt that their willingness to involve and inform officials in all issues – and not just the hospital closure – helped to reduce the likelihood of industrial action against the closure.

In these organizations, managers had been slowly creating a culture in which the level of trust between employees and employers was increased. In effect, they had been shaping an environment which would be more conducive to the changes that would be demanded by retrenchment (Hardy & Pettigrew, 1985). These experiences contrast quite sharply with those at Northville and Andersons. Managers at Northville had a history of ignoring unions and other groups, refusing to share information, and cutting services without consultation. The resulting animosity and suspicion undoubtedly contributed to the motivation to fight the Maine Road closure. Andersons' U.K. managers were concerned about their inability to pave the way for the announcement of the feasibility study. They were informed by headquarters management only a few weeks before employees were told of possible job losses. As a result, they were unable to do anything to change the militant nature of the works before the threat of job loss was made public, which increased the possibility of resistance.

Incorporating human resource considerations into long-term planning helps to avoid some of the problems that can be encountered during cutbacks. The problem is that human resource managers may lack the necessary power to play such a central, proactive role. The following section discusses some of the steps that can be taken to promote human resource management.

Promoting Human Resource Management

The effective involvement of human resource management can help to change a politically contentious situation to one in which the chances of opposition to cutbacks are minimized, and the chances of successful implementation maximized. Conversely, relegating human resources to a purely administrative function reduces the opportunities for successful retrenchment. What, then, can human resource managers do to ensure that they play a more active – and more successful – role in retrenchment?

Create Awareness in Senior Levels

One of the first steps human resource managers should take is to create awareness of the nature of the problem at senior levels. Senior management needs to be convinced that the time, effort, and expense involved in accommodating employee needs is worthwhile. There are a number of reasons, which have already been mentioned, that can be used. They revolve around the importance of survival; and the need to avoid obstacles such as union resistance, low morale, litigation, adverse publicity, and political intervention, which could jeopardize it. Similarly, human resource managers can point to the beneficial outcomes that are produced by a more enlightened approach to downsizing: productivity can increase; conflict can be reduced; favourable attitudes to management can be created. By employing effective persuasion, human resource managers must convince senior management that retrenchment is an investment, worth the expense necessary to accommodate employee needs and requiring the active involvement of the human resource function.

Human resource managers at Air Canada took steps to persuade senior executives of the need for action. The experience of the American airline industry with recession and deregulation was "powerful ammunition" in this respect. It enabled them to convince senior management that cost cutting should begin as soon as possible, while there was time to plan a more humane program than had been the case in most of the American companies.

Create Awareness Throughout the Organization

Human resource managers can also help to create an awareness of the need for cutbacks and their human resource implications at the lower levels. It will be important, particularly for union officials and stewards, to be convinced of the needs for cuts, if they are to accept them. The normal communication channels between human resource personnel and employee representatives can provide an arena in which discussions around the cutbacks can take place. Human resource managers can also use their knowledge of the personalities and issues involved to guide negotiations and discussions.

Plan Ahead

The early consideration of cutbacks is necessary so that alternative strategies can be considered and the details of downsizing worked out.

It is up to human resource managers to plan for the rundown. Cutbacks often cause problems because the organization is unfamiliar with the problem. Human resource managers must emphasize that they have the experience which underlies a successful retrenchment program. They have often been involved in previous downsizing programs or other change efforts, which can provide a useful basis for action. ICI used reports of closures in other divisions as well as its experience of other change programs. Managers documented the Mountside closure for future reference. CIL had carried out a number of plant closures, enabling human resource managers to compile a set of general guidelines for handling layoffs. Air Canada had undergone traumatic cutbacks in the early 1970s, which managers had no intention of repeating and which showed human resource managers what *not* to do. They used their "gloom and doom" files associated with an earlier downsizing exercise to plan this one.

Be Knowledgeable

Human resource managers know most about the political nature of the problem. They are familiar, for example, with the history of employee relations in the unit in question, the strike record, the profile of the workforce, the age and service characteristics, the alternative job opportunities. These factors have important implications for the way in which the retrenchment exercise should be implemented, for two reasons. First, this knowledge shows whether employee and union groups are likely to be able, or inclined, to contest managerial plans. Human resource managers, therefore, can ascertain at which groups actions should be directed. Second, the particular circumstances of the employees should be accommodated with packages that are tailor-made to their needs.

The old, long-serving workforces at the two British factory closures led to a traditional redundancy compensation package, which rewarded both these characteristics. CIL, on the other hand, had relatively young employees with short-service records, and so offered a $4,000 minimum to all individuals. The absence of alternative jobs results in a demand for outplacement aid. CIL provided aid because of the isolated nature of the community. AECL tried to find jobs for employees because of the depressed nature of the industry. The history of employee – management relations influences the chances of success, as Northville clearly shows. A history of union militancy makes a smooth closure harder to achieve, a factor which worried managers at Andersons and CIL. Redundancies which affect managerial or non-unionized staff may require different programs than those directed at employees who are covered by collective agreements.

It is the human resource managers who know the answers to these questions and who, as a result, have the clearest picture of the human and political dimension of the problem: which are the powerful interest groups that may obstruct implementation; how the debilitating effects of retrenchment may alienate continuing employees and jeopardize turnaround; and how best to accommodate these groups. Their active participation is, therefore, crucial to successful retrenchment if potentially disruptive interest groups are to be identified and accommodated.

Learn to Sell Human Resource Management

Effective retrenchment is more likely to occur when human resource management has high credibility and a large amount of power within the organization. Where this was the case in the studies, such as ICI, Whitefields, and Air Canada, the argument for a benevolent approach to retrenchment was well respected.

> We don't have any difficulty in making our points. I think we have the clout [power] we need (human resource executive at Air Canada).

In some cases, however, human resource management may be more vulnerable. At CIL it was a central staff function, designed only to advise. The decision-making prerogative was decentralized in the hands of line managers who may or may not have chosen to take their advice. In this particular closure, however, the status of human resource management was not a problem, because line management was determined to approach it humanely. The resulting coalition of line and human resource management had no problem in convincing senior management of the need for a program that accommodated employee and union interests. At AECL, human resource management had a much lower status and, as a result, more problems in influencing the retrenchment program. Many people felt that the refusal of the company to consider alternative strategies, and particularly voluntary dismissals, stemmed from a lack of power on the part of the human resource department.

Ideally, human resource management should be integrated into the strategy-making process (see, for example, Angle et al., 1985; Baird et al., 1983; Berger & Glass, 1983; Dyer, 1983; Ferris et al., 1984; Galosy, 1983; MacMillan & Schuler, 1985; McQueen, 1983; Miles & Snow, 1984). It increases the possibility of avoiding redundancies. At Whitefields, where such a situation existed, conservative hiring policies, subcontracting, temporary staff, and overtime provide the company with a series of buffers which enable it to have a full employment practice. It demands, however, a willingness to devote considerable time and effort to human resource issues.

Human resource management has, however, rarely managed to achieve such a high status as at Whitefields, as a result of inadequate power, and of practices that are rarely perceived to result in direct financial gains for the company (Jain & Murray, 1984). Ironically, retrenchment represents an opportunity to rectify both these weaknesses. First, with retrenchment becoming a common managerial challenge, and with the increasing emphasis on productivity and creativity from the employees who remain, effective human resource management is becoming a valued commodity. Managers must exploit it to enhance their power reserves. Second, as the experiences of the organizations in this study clearly demonstrate, the practices which relate to the enlightened handling of retrenchment do indeed produce visible benefits for the organization. Laying off people with a few hours notice and no support, on the other hand, can have numerous negative side effects. Human resource managers can use their successes with retrenchment to increase their credibility, by showing that their recommendations do, indeed, pay off.

Human resource managers who take the steps described here will not only be able to successfully manage retrenchment. They may also be able to take advantage of the opportunity to change narrow-minded and short-sighted attitudes: to promote the recognition that effective human resource management is an integral part of successful businesses.

Summary and Conclusions

This chapter has examined the implementation process and suggested steps that might be taken to smooth the process in order to increase the likelihood of both successful implementation, and sustain the commitment and motivation that will be necessary for the future success of the organization. It has focussed on the role of the human resource manager, to whom will fall much of the responsibility for introducing a broader and longer-term perspective into retrenchment. These steps have been deemed necessary because of the political component of cutbacks. Because resources are declining, it has been argued that one can expect to see conflict arise around the issue of downsizing. Such conflict might manifest itself in opposition to cutbacks, alienation on the part of remaining employees, or intervention by other interest groups. The next chapter examines the nature of opposition to cutbacks in more detail.

Chapter 13: Retrenchment and Resistance

This chapter examines the role of resistance in retrenchment decisions. It has been argued that the existence of reduced resources increases the chances of opposition to cutback from a variety of sources – employees, unions, managers, community groups, and politicians.

> In case of a serious resource reduction influencers who have hitherto been able to reach a stable equilibrium ... who were more or less satisfied with the distribution of pay-offs – suddenly find themselves in conflict with each other as each tries to maintain his or her share of a diminished pie (Mintzberg, 1983: 435–6).

Resistance illustrates the political nature of retrenchment, which has been emphasized throughout this book. It often represents the inability of employers to accommodate interest groups which, as a result, use the power at their disposal to influence the retrenchment process. Resistance can come from a number of sources. This chapter examines the phenomenon of union resistance and the more broadly based opposition found in the public sector. It then goes on to discuss the relationship between management and resistance – managers engaging in it, as well as fighting against it.

The Incidence of Resistance

There is a history of union resistance to retrenchment, particularly in the U.K. (see Hardy, 1985a). It was sparked by the beginning of the recession in the early 1970s. The U.K. endured the lowest growth rate in the western world between 1973 and 1979. Unemployment rose almost continuously through the decade, passing the one million mark in 1975 and reaching two million in 1980. In the context of this declining economy and an increased incidence of layoffs and closures, the first half of the 1970s saw a concerted effort on the part of union and employee groups to resist cutback decisions.

There were some 200 occupations protesting factory closures between 1970 and 1975, involving 150,000 workers. The occupation was considered a more effective weapon than a strike because it prevented the sale of assets, thereby putting pressure on the employers. A strike in the case of a firm closing down completely, it has been argued, has a minimal impact. The early 1970s were also notable for the founding of a number of worker cooperatives: Upper Clyde Shipbuilders (UCS) in 1971; Fakenham in 1972; Meriden in 1973; Kirkby in 1972 and 1974; the Scottish Daily News in 1975. These worker-led organizations emerged out of occupations, when the original owners sold the company, leaving employees, with government aid, to run it for themselves. It was the founding of UCS, after a well-publicized occupation, that initiated the increase in the use of the occupation.

The fact that these new tactics were limited to relatively small numbers should not detract from their importance – they also mobilized widespread support from other sources. The campaign to save UCS, for example, involved 100,000 stopping work and 50,000 joining a demonstration in Glasgow. Two months later there were 200,000 strikers and 80,000 marchers (Greenwood, 1977). UCS also attracted support from the media, the public, government, local members of parliament, other unions, and the Trades Union Congress.

The incidence of overt resistance to closures and layoffs appeared to decline in the late 1970s (Hardy, 1985 b). Fewer sit-ins were publicized, and the worker cooperative was no longer a symbol of the fight against redundancy. Nevertheless, there have been examples of opposition such as the campaigns against the closure of various steel works by the British Steel Corporation (Bryer et al., 1982), and the year-long strike by the National Union of Miners (NUM) in 1984 to prevent pit closures.

The example of the two health authorities shows that resistance can emerge from sources other than unions. At Midville, the recommendation to close Withybrooke, while accepted by the Area Health Authority (AHA), was opposed by the Community Health Council (CHC), which was supported by district and parish councils. It resulted in the decision being passed up to the Secretary of State who did not give his approval until March 1979. The matter has not finished even then, because a new government came into office, which did not give its approval until September 1979.

Resistance at Northville was even stronger, despite a general commitment to the principle of rationalizing maternity beds. The initial plan to close Maine Road caused hospital staff to set up an action committee to stop the closure. They wrote to general practitioners, lobbied members of parliament, appeared on television and radio, spoke at a local trades council meeting, contacted the press, and presented the chairman of the AHA with a petition of 10,000 signatures opposing it. They were supported by the CHC and the largest union (NUPE). Management's proposal to speed up the closure merely added fuel to the fire. The local media continued to report on the issue. The CHC and the unions continued to oppose the closure, and a consultant obstetrician from the hospital spoke out against it on medical grounds. An outburst of indignation arose from the staff at the hospital about the low turnout at a special meeting of the AHA, called to discuss it. Another meeting of the AHA finally overturned the closure proposal completely.

The example of Ville Marie shows an attempt by management to contest a cutback decision imposed on them by the government. The board initially refused to submit a plan for cuts of $2.3 million, substituting one for cuts of less than $250,000. The minister was not persuaded to reduce the budget cut, however, and the board eventually decided to comply with this request for a cutback plan, although some board members resigned in protest.

It is clear, then, that resistance arises in both public and private sectors. In the private sector, when resistance has occurred, it has tended to be, primarily, a union initiative. In the public sector, it often involves a wide number of different interest groups, including management. How do interest groups fight retrenchment decisions? It requires access to two forms of power: the objective ability to mobilize resources; and the subjective commitment of the individuals concerned to take such action (Hardy, 1985 b; Hyman & Fryer, 1975). In other words, power involves both the ability and the will to resist.

Union Resistance

The ability to resist is determined by structural sources of power. Where employees are concerned, a highly unionized workforce is an important source of structural power. It is able to disrupt production or engage in other activities which put pressure on management. Also important is the existence of official support for the actions taken by employees and shop stewards, and effective communication between these levels. Support on a wider basis – other unions, the Trades Union Congress, the Canadian Labour Congress, the American Federation of Labour, the broader labour movement, the media, and the public – reinforces attempts to resist managerial decisions. Another determinant of power concerns the strategic position of the workers in question – how easily they are able to disrupt production. For example, print workers are in a powerful position because of the perishability of their product, assembly line workers can bring an entire plant to a standstill.

In addition to these structural sources of power, employees must possess subjective power – the will and commitment to challenge managerial authority. In other words, they must perceive the situation – in this case, retrenchment – to be a conflict of interest. They must also feel that resistance is a feasible means of improving the situation, and be willing to engage in it.

In summary, it helps if employees are unionized, and have strong support from the higher echelons. In addition, strong leadership is often needed at the local level. Communication has to be established with other sympathetic groups and with employees in other localities. Opposition groups need to acquire as much information as they can to discredit management's case for closure, and they should use the media effectively to promote public and political support (Levie et al., 1984).

It would appear, however, that unions and employees face considerable difficulty in contesting layoffs and closures. One problem seems to be a general weakening of union power in recent years. In addition, there are specific difficulties in fighting retrenchment decisions. It would appear that both the structural and subjective sources of union power have diminished (Hardy, 1985 b).

This phenomenon is most clearly seen in the U.K. The resistance of the early 1970s can be associated with an increase in union power. Union membership rose, while inflation and the threat of increased unemployment produced a concern for the protection of living standards. The number of working days lost due to pay claims rose, which indicates attempts to protect wages. Wage increases exceeded inflation during the early part of the decade. Employees also took steps to protect themselves against increasing unemployment. The occupations and worker cooperatives have been explained as pragmatic approaches to the degenerating economic climate, which was reducing the chances of finding alternative employment, and making it imperative to hold on to existing jobs (Bradley, 1978; Buchan, 1972).

As the 1970s progressed and the 1980s commenced, this militancy declined. Unemployment increased and union membership decreased, robbing employees of an important structural source of power. While the threat of unemployment tends to increase union membership, because workers try to protect themselves from potential job loss, numbers fall when the job losses become a reality (Price & Bain, 1983). The same may be said of the effect on union militancy (Bright et al., 1983; Edwards, 1982). A similiar situation has occurred in North America where union membership has declined from 33 per cent in the 1950s to less than 20 per cent. In Canada, union membership was recently at a sixteen-year low.

Another factor to consider concerns government strategies and policies. With the election of the Labour Party in 1974, a new industrial policy was created to regenerate British industry. It was, however, aimed at national union leaders, who were drawn into negotiations to support sectoral strategies. These strategies often involved specific closures, as with, for example, the British Steel Corporation and British Leyland. Localized attempts to stave off job losses often suffered from a lack of support. Union leaders were in no position to support local resistance campaigns because of their commitment to the broader economic policy. In addition, local officials suffered from a lack of direct communication with the government, which was confining its negotiations to national union leaders (for example, Beynon, 1973; Beynon & Wainwright, 1979; Bryer et al., 1982; Ursell, 1976). So, despite a government which was supposedly supportive of the labour movement, its economic policies inadvertently made it harder to resist layoffs at the local level.

Since the election of the Conservative government in 1979, government policies have been directed explicitly towards the weakening of union power (Ball, 1985; Soskice, 1985; Unwin & Murray, 1983). These policies have been manifested in legislation, an unwillingness to intervene in industrial disputes, and a tough line on the part of government.

As a result, national unions have failed to provide effective opposition or constructive alternatives to closures and redundancies. Even the miners' strike was eventually defeated, with the union gaining little in the way of concessions. The attitude of the government concerning unions is similar in the U.S. and the election of the Progressive Conservatives in Canada is unlikely to add significantly to union power.

Finally, there is the question of the managerial strategies that have weakened union power. Employers have reinforced political and economic influences by using the continued recession to change perceptions of the legitimacy of closure. In the early 1970s, closures and redundancies were not deemed legitimate; a society that has previously emphasized growth and full employment finds it difficult to accept closure, redundancies, and unemployment. Layoffs leave people without jobs, unions without members, and communities without services. It is not surprising, then, that such actions were considered illegitimate, as evidenced by the resistance of employee and union groups, and the intervention of the government in the case of the worker cooperatives.

More recently, however, managers have been able to redefine redundancy to make it more acceptable. A number of efforts by companies (for example, the British Steel Corporation and Courtaulds) to explain and justify their actions have been documented (Hardy, 1985 b). This continual justification of redundancies on the grounds of economic, technical, and commercial criteria makes them more acceptable – they become considered as necessary or even desirable. It reinforces the values implicit in public policy which has defined the problem in managerial terms – not that redundancy is undesirable and should be eliminated – but how best to facilitate managerial decision making, and encourage workers to accept the inevitability and desirability of redundancy (Fryer, 1973). The redundancy fund established in 1965 to provide compensation was established on the basis that severance payments would increase mobility and reduce resistance to change.

Closure has thus become a fact of life. If closure is viewed as necessary, justifiable, or inevitable, doubt is then cast on the legitimacy of opposition. It makes it harder to maintain support for and commitment to resistance. Whereas redundancy was contested in the early 1970s because it was viewed as socially and morally undesirable; towards the latter part of the decade, closure came to be defined as an economic necessity. It meant that opposition groups had to demonstrate rational, technical, or commercial reasons why rationalization should *not* occur.

In North America, other managerial strategies are weakening union power. Many companies are relocating plants in areas of non-unionized labour (Bolle, 1980; Harrison, 1984; Kochan et al., 1984). Also two-tier levels of employees have been created – full time and temporary –, the latter without the protections and benefits afforded to permanent unionized employees. These changes and the effects of the recession have reduced union power and helped to account for some of the wage concessions that have been negotiated, not all of which may have been warranted on an economic basis (Ruben, 1984).

In addition to these general influences which reduce the likelihood of resistance, there are the specific difficulties of fighting particular cutbacks. Unions often lack the information and the resources to fully analyze management's arguments. With their access to data, it is relatively easy for employers to "prove" that an individual plant or operation is unprofitable. Employees often learn of layoffs when it is too late to do anything, since the decision has already been taken. Managers can block attempts to extend action by arguing that resistance will jeopardize jobs in other parts of the organization – playing different unions and employee groups off against each other. "Downing tools" (stopping work) can play into employers' hands, enabling them to make the layoffs more quickly.

The very measures recommended in the early chapters to ease the process of retrenchment for employees also serve to reduce the likelihood of resistance (Hardy, 1985 a). First, the benefits provided by the organization are, implicitly or explicitly, dependent on acquiescence to the closure. Employees are reluctant to compromise those benefits, particularly their severance pay, by taking action against the closure. Second, the fact that management is being cooperative and helpful to employees makes it difficult to engender support among the public, politicians, and other groups, which see the organization acting in a benevolent and socially responsible manner.

What, then, can unions do to protect their employees in the face of layoffs? Some writers have argued that employees and unions should fight layoffs, for a number of different reasons. There is the chance to win; people feel better if they have tried to fight; a great deal is learnt in the process; it provides alternatives to closures and layoffs (Levie et al., 1984) and may save some jobs. Stewards may have more power than they realize. At ICI, for example, resistance might have procured an even more generous redundancy package. The stewards agreed to the company's offer, although management later admitted that, if necessary, it would probably have been prepared to negotiate a more generous settlement.

> What the stewards and officials wouldn't have appreciated is how worried the company was that the closure shouldn't go wrong. Because the company was worried, if the officials had made a big thing of it and said "Fine, you close a works down but we're going to negotiate something special for that", the company would have negotiated so as to prevent trouble and the possibility of it spreading and affecting our business (manager).

There are, however, risks with a confrontational route: the fight may not be won; and benefits and severance pay may be lost. U.K. managers at Andersons argued, for example, that a strike or occupation would simply have led to an earlier closure, without Merryvale to save 200 jobs.

The dilemma is, then, whether to risk overt confrontation. Resistance may fail for a number of reasons: insufficient power sources; an unwillingness to fight; it may be totally ineffective if the organization is in such a poor financial position that it has no other option than to go ahead with cutbacks; it may result in management reducing severance pay and eliminating any attempts to save jobs. Failing to fight, on the other hand, can result in the loss of benefits that the company might have been willing to concede under pressure. Ideally, union officials would have sufficient information about the organization's situation, and sufficient power to take the appropriate course of action – a rare occurrence.

Resisting layoffs is, then, a difficult business. Recent developments in both the U.K. and North America would appear to have weakened union power in this respect. Employees and officials need to carefully consider their chances of success before embarking on resistance. It can be used to negotiate a better deal for the employees who are laid off and, in some cases at least, prevent closure. In other cases, union officials may be serving the needs of their members more effectively by acquiescing to layoffs, and not risking the loss of severance payments.

Resistance in the Public Sector

In the public sector a broader set of external and internal constituencies may exist. Managerial functions are often divided between some sort of board and management. The board usually has the ultimate decision-making power, although it may not choose to exercise it. Public boards consist of people from a variety of backgrounds with their own constituencies and interests. This diversity was particularly evident in the NHS, where board members represented such groups as employees, unions, professionals, the public, and local politicians. The viewpoint of individual board members varies according to their commitments to, and dependency on, their constituencies. The councillors on Northville Area Health Authority (AHA), for example, were particularly sensitive to public opinion because of the balance of power in local government, which made them keen to support causes that would win them electoral votes.

There may also be a variety of external interest groups. At Northville, the resistance involved a coalition of key doctors, nurses, other employees, the unions, and the Community Health Council (CHC). There may be opponents of cutbacks in the various levels of the bureaucracy and in the government. Local politicians with constituencies in the area may take a different stand to the cabinet minister responsible for the portfolio. Government positions may change. Midville illustrates this point. The formal objection by the CHC passed the decision up to the minister, a member of a Conservative government that had been recently elected on the basis of a cost-conscious manifesto. His support for the closure decision was in keeping with it. Over time, however, the government's position changed, and the Conservatives started to favour small community hospitals. Management believed it would have been very difficult to secure support for the closure had the issue arisen later, even though the government was continuing to restrict public funding.

Structural power – the ability to resist – in the public sector will depend on identifying the various interest groups, and establishing whether they are supportive of resistance or not. It will also depend on being able to build effective alliances and coalitions with these groups. Choices have to be made as to which groups should be included to help further the cause, and which should be confined to a less visible role. Obviously, those with power and influence should be included.

One such group in the case of the hospital closures was the doctors – because of their perceived expertise, they had considerable influence on both the AHA and the public. Northville doctors opposed the closure and were instrumental in the case for retention. Doctors at Midville, in contrast, did not oppose the decision. Other groups may be powerful because of their numbers. Local councillors make up one-third of the AHA membership so that "if they decide to turn up in force, they can reverse any decision".

Groups which might alienate, rather than create, support will have to be excluded. Opposition groups at Northville decided not to openly affiliate themselves with the unions.

> I didn't want the CHC to get involved with the unions. ... I wanted to make sure that I looked at it from the view of the patients (CHC secretary).

As a result, the unions, while supportive of the campaign, kept a low profile.

> If we had fought it our way, I think we would have lost the sympathy of the general public (shop steward).

Union involvement, on the other hand, can be an advantage, as at Ville Marie where they were an active part of the resistance.

The institution has to decide whether to solicit the support of similar organizations or to plead on its own behalf. Ville Marie chose to act alone which, some have argued, was self-defeating. Alone, Ville Marie lacked sufficient power to put effective pressure on the government. A coalition with Montréal Métropolitain – the francophone agency – might have strengthened them. Also, the defence of a relatively small anglophone institution, representing what is perceived to be a relatively privileged sector in a francophone province, lacked political feasibility. Ville Marie might have been more effective in its fight against the cuts if it had joined forces with other organizations, and had broadened the issue to a more politically acceptable concern regarding the funding of all social welfare agencies.

Support from potential coalition members is not automatic, it has to be mobilized by creating the will to fight. The key is to delegitimize the cutbacks, by creating legitimacy for the organization and its mission in the eyes of the various stakeholders. Different strategies may have to be directed at each group.

Public support can be attracted through the media and public meetings. It seems that arguments that appeal to emotions rather than clinical arguments, are more effective here. For example, Maine Road received considerable support because of its age and history – its survival during the war.

> Once you make it a technical question you lose the public ... you don't talk about *per capitas* (board member at Ville Marie).
>
> People form parochial attachments. They have an emotional and not a clinical view (consultant at Northville).

It is important to recognize which arguments are deemed legitimate by the relevant interest groups and which are not. In the public sector, financial reasons may not be considered an acceptable basis on which to curtail services. At Midville, managers were careful to secure medical approval for the closure so that, while much needed cost saving would be one result, there were no medical grounds on which to contest the closure. At Northville, in contrast, management's financial criteria were not accepted, and medical arguments for the closure were contested by doctors who opposed it.

Any claim for increased resources directed at the government will have to be accompanied by rational argumentation and quantitative data to support the case. While political arguments and public sentiment provide some influence, political decisions are at least validated with reference to the "facts" – i. e., data that are marshalled to justify the outcome (Fox, 1978; Majone, 1976/7; Meltsner, 1972; Sabatier, 1978; Weiss & Bucuvalas, 1980). Such data may also be needed to cultivate support among other interest groups. Ville Marie's attempt to resist the cutbacks was undermined by its inability to play the numbers "game". Learning from experience, Ville Marie now has "a position paper that is really well documented with good solid arguments".

Political strategies, which involve the creation of legitimacy, the building of coalitions, and the nurturing of support require:

> *savoir faire* and knowledge of dealing with the mechanisms of the bureaucracy. ... You have to participate in the system and all the informal lobbying that goes on (Ville Marie board member).

Managerial Resistance

Managerial resistance would appear to be more common in the public sector. It has been argued that managers will often take steps to resist cuts before they implement them (Levine, 1979; Jick & Murray, 1982). It is not to say that individual managers in business do not contest their budgets or try to influence resource allocation decisions, but they have, rarely, openly joined overt opposition campaigns against closure and layoff decisions. Budget cuts in the public sector are imposed on managers by governments and are determined by political considerations, rather than by profit and loss (Hardy, 1985 b). It raises the question of whether management should openly resist cutbacks if they can muster effective support. The decision of whether to resist is not, however, as simple as it sounds – there are a number of pitfalls associated with managerial resistance.

Managerial resistance can create problems, particularly if resources are not increased and the cuts still have to be implemented. Resistance increases uncertainty, simply because the campaign may be successful in reducing or avoiding cuts. Until the outcome is known, this uncertainty can be counterproductive; "not knowing" may be more uncomfortable than "knowing the worst". Organizations that delay the cuts while the resistance campaign is being mounted, can find themselves ultimately faced with larger cuts in order to balance the budget. If an organization is to cultivate support, it will have to paint the worst picture regarding the impact of cutbacks which creates considerable uncertainty. Ville Marie projected the loss of eighty-four posts, although only twenty-two people actually lost their jobs.

Further uncertainty accompanies the question of how far to go in resisting cuts. Had Ville Marie continued to refuse to implement the funding cuts, it would have run the risk of being placed in trusteeship, whereby the government would have taken over the functions of the board.

> I thought it was good that someone took a stand, but at the same time I didn't know what it would do. We were afraid that if they [the board members] all resigned we'd be placed into trusteeship, and people were more afraid of trusteeship (employee).

The board eventually decided to comply with the minister's demand for a cutback plan. That decision produced criticism from employees who felt that the board should have taken a stronger stand.

> The government expects you to scream and yell. The board should have *refused* to cut. Many of us were ready to accept trusteeship ... we compromise and compromise until there's nothing left (union representative).

The united front of management and unions at Ville Marie placed a severe strain on the union representatives who, while supporting actions which might prevent the cuts, were worried that they were being excluded from the process of deciding where the cuts would be made.

> The unions couldn't attack the hypothetical plans on cutbacks without discrediting the organization which was fighting to minimize cuts. So they weren't able to operationalize their part of the strategy until later on when cuts became a reality. ... The union wasn't stupid, and they realized they were being manipulated, but they had no choice: their interests were really Ville Marie's interests, and they couldn't get to the second level of their strategy which was in terms of getting to that management process of how cuts were structured within the Centre (board member).

Union members and managers who resist also run the risk of incurring blame if their efforts fail.

> From my point of view, they [the unions] didn't do as much as they could have done. ... They had the most power to fight cutbacks (Ville Marie manager).

Finally, there is the question of whether the effort is worth it. Northville provides one example of successful resistance. Elsewhere, however, the picture is different: opposition in Midville failed to prevent the closure; and Ville Marie still had to sustain an 11 per cent cut. Opposition can also backfire, alienating the government and perhaps jeopardizing future relations, and losing public support.

Despite the pitfalls discussed above, there are, nevertheless, some advantages to be derived from managerial opposition. First, the legitimacy that is created for the organization and its mission in the eyes of the public, and the attention that is drawn to the damage done by funding restrictions, can help to protect the institution in the longer term. Furthermore, the education that occurs through the marshalling of data can help to change future government policies.

If cuts can be reduced or delayed, the organization gains time to find access to other sources of funding. Miles & Cameron (1982) refer to these delaying tactics as domain defence. The legitimacy of the existing mission of the enterprise is defended, allowing the examination of other solutions such as increased market penetration (domain offense) and diversification (domain creation). These strategies were observed in the tobacco industry when it was first threatened by health concerns. Cameron (1983) has since applied the model to universities where political lobbying is used to delay threats to the organization's existence, and to allow new techniques to be used to attract students, increase enrolment, or solicit funds from private sources.

Resistance to cutbacks can be important for administrators because of the symbolic effect of such an effort. Managers and administrators who fight cuts will be viewed as having a commitment to the organization, its employees, and its clients. It is particularly important for managerial credibility and may, ironically, help the subsequent implementation of cuts, if employees feel their managers did all they could to prevent them. If resistance is going to occur from other quarters anyway, managers have to seriously consider whether they ought not to join it. At Northville, resistance ended up being directed against management and, when the closure was rescinded, managers found themselves having to do a 180-degree turn, with their credibility severely compromised.

There are, then, a number of advantages associated with the strategy of resistance; not least is the very real possibility of avoiding or reducing cutbacks. Political strategies to resist cuts represent a viable course of action that managers and administrators should seriously consider. Notwithstanding this, there are some pitfalls of which managers must be aware, if they are to make an intelligent choice and avoid the associated problems.

Management Against Resistance

While managers may engage in resistance, their more common role is one of implementing retrenchment decisions. The case studies clearly show that success depends upon identifying the potential opposition groups and devising a strategy that deals with their concerns. In this way, conflict is preempted (Hardy, 1985 a, 1985 c) and the chances of successful implementation increased. Failing to recognize powerful opponents or ignoring their existence can result in a battle in which management is the loser. This situation can be clearly seen in the comparison of the two hospital closures (Hardy, 1986d).

Managerial actions were quite different in these two case studies. Midville managers had approached the closure anxious that nothing should jeopardize their plans. They were aware that a number of groups had the potential to do so; including the Area Health Authority (AHA) that had to vote on the management's recommendation; the Community Health Council (CHC) whose objection could produce ministerial intervention; and the public and the unions who, if they chose to protest against the closure, could put pressure on either the AHA, through the local councillors who were often sensitive to public opinion, or the minister. Management was, then, reluctant to risk overt confrontation with any of these groups, for fear that it could jeopardize their plans.

The first step was to ensure the unions did not resist the closure, and, to do this, full consultation was used. Management also offered all employees of the hospital the choice between redundancy with compensation or a similar, new job as far as it was possible. These actions built credibility for management, providing an indication that they were trying to accommodate employee needs.

Another step that management took was to justify their decision to close the hospital. It was particularly important in relation to the AHA, which had ultimate responsibility for deciding on the strategy and, therefore, had to be convinced it was necessary. They did so by blaming the closure on the government's budget cuts, impressing upon all interest groups the vital need for the closure to safeguard other services. It not only legitimized the strategy, but also conveniently absolved management of all blame, even though the hospital would still have closed as a result of rationalization plans.

Another interest group that merited particular attention was the doctors. The use of profit and loss criteria are not always perceived as legitimate reasons for the withdrawal of services, and medical opposition can easily override any financial arguments in the eyes of the public, employees and unions, the AHA, and often the government. In this case, management was careful not to antagonize them, having offered, in compensation, new wards in another hospital.

The final result was that, despite CHC opposition, the chances of resistance had been minimized, and the likelihood that the minister would support the decision maximized. As expected, the minister supported management's choice of strategy and, although the decision was delayed by the CHC protest, even this was turned to a political advantage.

> We rather hoped the CHC would oppose it as this would help us in our fight for more money [from the government] (manager).

Northville was not characterized by the same type of political awareness. Management had already been criticized for its previous bad handling of sensitive issues and its poor relations with the powerful unions. As a result, management had contributed to an already factionalized situation. In addition, management made a number of tactical errors in dealing with the various interest groups during the closure process.

Management did not recognized the emotional appeal of the hospital. When the staff of the hospital formed an action committee to fight the proposed closure, they secured the support of the general public and the media. Management, on the other hand, failed to make use of the media to argue their case.

> Senior management did not make use of the press. They thought that a rational debate in the council chamber would suffice (manager).

They missed an opportunity to split public opinion by failing to point out that if Maine Road did not close, wards in other hospitals would. Management failed to secure the support of the doctors – all the vocal ones opposed the closure.

> The fact that a senior consultant obstetrician was speaking for the retention of Maine Road went a long way towards the campaign's success (manager).

Management might have been able to muster more medical support had they countered the argument that the hospital was too good a specialist unit to be closed, and by pointing out that maternity units within larger general hospitals with all their support and back-up facilities were much safer. It was a view held by the government and had been the subject of a number of reports on the health service (such as the 1962 Hospital Plan and the 1967 Bonham-Carter report).

Management tried to use financial criteria to justify the closure of the hospital. It was not, however, a politically adept move in a city noted for its deprivation and poverty, particularly as management had already been blamed for previous cuts in service. Financial exigencies were simply not considered legitimate grounds by many of the interest groups on which to rationalize the reduction of services. The end result was that the AHA voted against the recommendation to close Maine Road, because management had failed to convince anyone that it was necessary or justifiable.

Conclusions

Resistance is a phenomenon that has occurred in tandem with many retrenchment decisions. Scarce resources lead to conflict which, in turn, can result in opposition campaigns. In the business world, this resistance has been primarily union/employee led. Such a resistance movement built up in the early 1970s, but died away during the latter part of the decade. The change in resistance patterns can be attributed to a decline in both the structural sources of power – the ability to resist – and the subjective sources – the will to resist – on the part of the larger trade union movement. Despite these broad trends, union resistance can still occur, as the 1984 miners' strike in the U.K. showed. Even if such overt opposition does not occur, resistance may take more subtle forms in the form of noncooperation. Resistance in the public sector often involves a larger number of interest groups and may incorporate management. Success depends on the same factors as with unions – the ability and will to resist. The former is acquired through coalition building; the latter by delegitimizing cutbacks.

The possibility of resistance means that managers have to develop a political awareness if they are to implement retrenchment plans successfully. The comparison of the two health authorities shows that managers at Midville were successful because they recognized and accommodated the interest groups that could interfere with its plan. Northville, on the other hand, failed to acknowledge these groups. The successful organizations in the study were those that realized that successful retrenchment was not just an economic matter but, if it was to be implemented, would require a political analysis of the various interest groups. Hence, CIL, ICI, Ville Marie, Andersons, and Whitefields were concerned about their employees and/or unions; while AECL and Air Canada were also anxious to maintain a low public profile.

It is not just retrenchment that requires political adroitness; other situations may provide the impetus for opponents to engage in political behaviour. If interest groups exist that have both the will and the ability to challenge managerial decisions, politics will become a matter of survival. The next chapter discusses this issue in more detail.

Chapter 14: The Politics of Survival

The previous chapter illustrated how various interest groups intervened in the retrenchment process. The reason they did so was because they possessed both subjective and objective sources of power (Hyman & Fryer, 1975). In other words, these stakeholders had both the motivation and the ability to challenge managerial decisions. It has been argued that cutbacks are particularly prone to such political pressures – because resources are declining, actors are motivated to engage in political activity in order to protect their interests. If they also possess sufficient power to influence the retrenchment process, managers may find their plans in jeopardy. It was precisely because of this threat, that retrenchment was deemed to be a political as well as an economic problem.

It would be naive to assume that cutbacks are the only issue that provokes political activity. A number of writers have, over the years, drawn our attention to the political nature of organizations (for example, Crozier, 1964; Cyert & March, 1963; Pettigrew, 1973; Pfeffer, 1981). There are, in fact, certain conditions that make organizations more prone to political activity, by increasing the likelihood that internal or external stakeholders are both inclined and able to intervene in the decision-making process. If such stakeholders exist, as the examples in this book have demonstrated, organizational survival will depend on strategies that cater to the political dimension of the problem, and not just the economic component. This political side of management is, however, often neglected in the traditional strategy-making literature, where the emphasis is usually on the development of analytic, rather than political, skills. Analysis may be of limited value, however, when strategy making resembles a political quagmire, rather than a series of rational, economic decisions.

This chapter examines these issues in more detail, using the organizations in the study to illustrate the arguments. In so doing, it broadens the focus from retrenchment strategies to strategy making in general. It explores the internal and external environments of organizations to show under which circumstances they become prey to political constraints. It develops a framework that can be applied to organizations, which helps them identify the nature of their political context. Finally, it draws some conclusions for the nature of strategy making under such conditions.

The Internal Political Environment

This section discusses some of the conditions under which internal interest groups will represent a political threat for managers. Much of this research has been carried out in the public sector. Despite differences between public and private sectors (for example, Smith Ring & Perry, 1985), there are enough similarities (Mintzberg & Jorgenson, 1987; Vickers, 1965) to make these findings relevant for business managers.

Goals and Criteria

Business organizations are traditionally considered to have one clearly defined goal – profit. Goals in the public sector are considered to be more problematic – diverse, unquantifiable, intangible, and conflicting (Rainey et al., 1976). They are often related to some concept of the "public interest", which is both difficult to define and has the habit of changing over time (Harmon, 1969). Ambiguous goals result in a lack of quantifiable criteria which can be used to measure progress and performance (Garrett, 1972), and there are few of the clear market indicators that supposedly guide the private sector (Rainey et al., 1976).

> Considerations of efficiency have to be traded off against other considerations such as equity ..., political and legal feasibility, administrative capacity and so on (Reuber, 1982: 11).

In reality, however, profit-making organizations may also have problematic goals. Cyert & March (1963) were among the first to draw attention to the fact that organizations consist of different interest groups, and that goals are likely to be a product of the dominant coalition of these groups.

> It is now a commonplace that organizations per se do not have goals. What we call goals are the products of a process of interaction and negotiation within the organization, and indeed across organizational boundaries (Walsh et al., 1981: 133).

Decision Making

The rational economic model framework, whereby managers optimize decisions, has long been replaced by models which take into account the complexity and nuances of decision making (for example, Simon, 1955). Consequently, the public administration literature is full of studies which have shown that decision making is anything but rational (see, for example, Dror, 1967; Gawthrop, 1971; Greenwood et al., 1976; Haywood, 1983; Heclo, 1972; Meltsner, 1972; Meyerson & Bamfield, 1955; Ukeles, 1977; Wildavsky, 1964). Studies of business decisions have also been found to be highly political (for example, Mumford & Pettigrew, 1975; Pettigrew, 1973).

Decision making will obviously be affected by confusion regarding goals and criteria. Under these circumstances, managers cannot easily control or direct decision making. "Good" decisions are difficult to identify, and progress towards them is hard to monitor. In the absence of the profit motive, managers will be unable to rely on the bottom line to guide and evaluate actions – qualitative and subjective decisions will become necessary. In the absence of clearly defined decision-making procedures, there is considerably more room for political activity.

Authority

Authority in the public sector is often fragmented (Rainey et al., 1976). For example, the boards of government agencies may represent a number of different external constituencies and wield considerable decision-making power, voting on managerial recommendations (Hardy, 1985 a, 1985 d; 1986 c). Under these circumstances, managers cannot simply impose decisions on the rest of the organization.

The stereotypical business enterprise is described as having clear top-down authority, and implicit in much of the prescriptive literature on strategy making is the idea that strategies are formulated at the top and implemented down through the organization.

> In industry, the owner-entrepreneur is a free agent within the law and even when ownership and management are separate it is rare for "accountability to the shareholder" to have any great force (Garret, 1972: 189).

Not all private enterprises can be said to correspond to this description, however. Mintzberg (1979) has identified professional bureaucracies and adhocracies, which are characterized by decentralized power. Due to the power of expertise, traditional authority patterns are circumvented by professionals and experts located lower in the hierarchy.

Interest Groups

Fragmented authority allows the emergence of competing interest groups, which are able to influence the decision-making process. They are particularly likely to be active during the formulation and implementation of strategy, since strategic decisions open up opportunities to gain additional resources, and threats to existing resource allocations (for example, Hardy, 1985 a, 1985 b; Kanter, 1983; Mumford & Pettigrew, 1975; Pettigrew 1973). The resulting dissension provides the motivation for coalition building around the planned changes, with the intention of shaping or blocking them (Huff, 1980; Pettigrew, 1976). If these interest groups are powerful, such as professionals in a professional bureaucracy, experts in an adhocracy, or unionized labour, they will be in a position to exercise a considerable amount of influence over the strategy making.

Certain organizations have, then, significant potential for political processes, particularly those that can be described as *factionalized* (*diagram 6*), by which we mean that, instead of groups who comply with managerial decisions, one or more factions exist, which contest these decisions. In factionalized organizations, ambiguous goals increase the chances of conflicts of interest between groups; unquantifiable criteria and ill-defined decision making provide the opportunity to play out political behaviour; the existence of dispersed authority and powerful, dissenting interest groups ensure that actors have both

Diagram 6: The Internal Political Environment

ambiguous	goals	unambiguous
unquantifiable	criteria	quantifiable
ill-defined	decision making	well-defined
dispersed	authority	top-down
powerful, dissentious	internal interest groups	powerless, consensual
Factionalized	The Organization	Compliant

the motivation and ability to make an impact. Decision making is thus characterized by coalitions (Stevenson et al., 1985), cleavage (Astley et al., 1982), and politicality (Hickson et al., 1986).

Factionalized organizations will find it more difficult to rely on a purely economic orientation when making decisions. This situation is exacerbated by certain types of decision – retrenchment is obviously one example. Strategic decision making is another example, because complexity and uncertainty make acceptable, standardized procedures harder to find, and changes in resource allocation patterns threaten interest groups. These factors undoubtedly account for the growing literature arguing that strategic decisions involve political processes (Aharoni, 1966; Carter, 1969; Child, 1972; Fahey 1981; King, 1976; Narayanan & Fahey, 1982; Pettigrew, 1977, 1985; Quinn, 1978, 1980).

The External Political Environment

Organizations are not only subject to intervention from internal interest groups – external stakeholders may be equally threatening to managerial decisions. This section discusses some of the conditions that give rise to external stakeholder activity.

Funding

Public organizations are usually publicly funded, rather than user supported, and as a result, their external dependency is clear. Many private organizations also rely on the public purse, however, through contracts, grants, tax incentives, and loans (Bozeman & Straussman, 1984). Some business organizations are dependent on outside funds from other sources. Subsidiaries may find themselves dependent on the corporate level for capital investment; others may require financing from other companies or financial institutions. In the event of external funding, the organization becomes dependent on these external stakeholders, which will have to be persuaded to give their support – a process that often requires courting and lobbying as much as economic arguments.

Accountability and Control

Public sector managers are usually accountable to parliamentary bodies or other government agencies (Baker, 1972; Bower, 1977; Hinings & Greenwood, 1973; Keeling, 1972; Rainey et al., 1976). It translates into a web of legal and formal controls that can affect all aspects of an organization's functioning. These controls come from a number of different interest groups, including the larger political network of civil servants, ministers, and parliament (Brown, 1970; Heclo & Wildavsky, 1974; Vickers, 1965). Private organizations in regulated industries may find themselves equally ineffective by rules and regulations (Birnbaum, 1985), and those reporting to conglomerates will have to conform to certain procedures.

Public Scrutiny

Public sector organizations often provide key goods or services which attract a considerable amount of public and media attention. Public decision making occurs in a "goldfish bowl", as external groups check to see whether public dollars have been well spent (Reuber, 1982). Such interest is also attached to private firms producing dangerous products, such as alcohol, nuclear power, and chemicals. Most of these industries have been the subject of intense public scrutiny at one time or another – as the examples of Mothers Against Drunk Drivers, the Three Mile Island incident, and the Bhopal tragedy clearly show. In fact, public scrutiny is a major issue in both North America and Europe as consumer, environmental, and other interest groups become an important source of pressure (Mintzberg, 1984 a). In such a situation, managers may find themselves as concerned with the public relations value of decisions as with their economic benefits.

External Interest Groups

Public scrutiny, external funding and control, and socially significant goals add up to a large number of external interest groups with both the power and the motivation to influence the organization. These political pressures are not confined to public organizations (Keim et al., 1984; Mintzberg, 1983); the autonomy of business is often overemphasized (Bozeman & Straussman, 1984). Miles & Cameron (1982) have shown how heavily influenced the tobacco industry has been – by Congress, the Federal Trades Commission, and the anti-smoking lobby. Influence does not just come from government sources – with mergers, acquisitions, takeovers, and conglomerates, a subsidiary may be just as constrained by its business stakeholders as is a government department by political mandarins.

> If one accepts a working definition of the "publicness" of resources as the degree of external control exerted by government entities, curious possibilities emerge: some firms are no less "public" than some government organizations (Bozeman & Straussman, 1984: 81).

External funding and control renders an organization accountable to external parties such as government agencies or conglomerates. In the event of high public scrutiny and products or services that are deemed to be of high social significance, the government, the public, and other consumer groups may be motivated to intervene. If these external groups are both active and powerful, the organization will find itself *besieged* by its stakeholders (*diagram 7*). Autonomous organizations, because of their political independence, are free to concentrate on economic strategies. The survival of besieged organizations, on the other hand, will depend on political actions.

> Any organization ... must deliver a product or service clients' demand but it must also engage in a political process of building support among sympathizers, other organizations and legislators (Randall, 1973: 236).

Managers of besieged organizations will, then, have to consider the management of legitimacy (Bozeman & Straussman, 1984; Dowling & Pfeffer, 1975; Meyer & Rowan, 1977/8; Pfeffer & Salancik, 1978),

Diagram 7: The External Political Environment

externally generated	funding	internally generated
external	control	internal
socially significant	goals	of no social significance
high	public scrutiny	low
powerful, active	external interest groups	powerless, passive
Besieged	The Organization	Autonomous

collective strategies (Astley & Fombrun, 1983), and other political strategies as lobbying, political action committees, constituency building, and advocacy building (Keim & Zeithaml, 1986).

The Nature of Political Constraints

We can explore the political nature of the internal and external environment more closely by examining the organizations in the study. Each of these organizations faced a different mix of political pressures and, so, was more or less factionalized and/or besieged (*diagram 8*).

Diagram 8: Political Constraints on the Retrenching Organizations

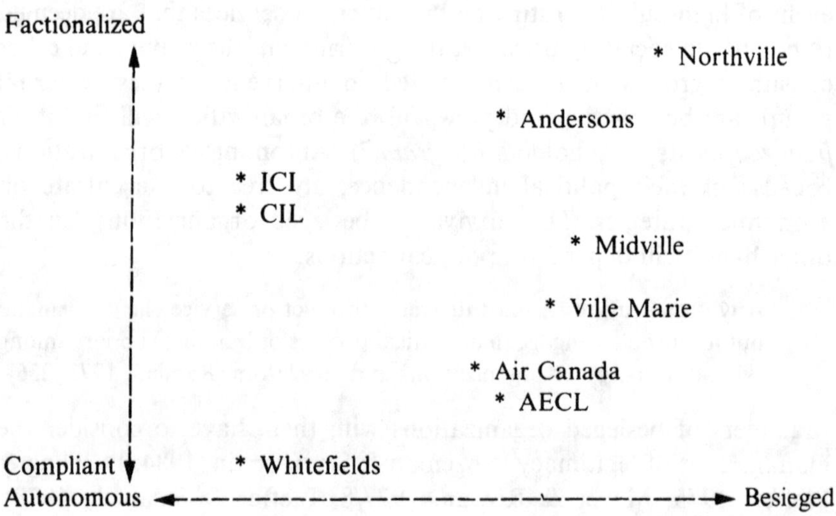

Whitefields was the only organization to be free of virtually all political pressures. It was a nonunionized organization, and so there was no union to challenge managerial decisions; nor was there any evidence of other internal interest groups. While the company is large and, as such, is involved in government contracts and attracts public attention, it, nevertheless, appeared to be free of external stakeholders with any major influence. Its only external concern, as far as the early retirement program was concerned, was to avoid media attention.

ICI and CIL were also relatively free of external political constraints, other than a similar desire to avoid media attention. They did, however, have one internal group to deal with: the union. Both organizations defined retrenchment as a political problem because of the threat of union resistance.

AECL and Air Canada, as crown corporations, were, to some extent, besieged by external stakeholders – primarily in the form of susceptibility to media attention and government intervention. Air Canada was slightly more autonomous, in that it operated on a commercial basis and relied on the government only for 40 per cent of its long-term debt. (This dependency on the government would appear to be increasing in the short term – the move towards privatization requires the support of the government and, if it fails, government financing will be required to fund the acquisition of new aircraft. In the long term, if privatization is achieved, the corporation should become more autonomous.) AECL relied on government appropriations to fund its research and development activities. In 1983, they exceeded $ 180 million – 28 per cent of total revenue. The government also provided loan financing of $ 7 million, and more than 90 per cent of the corporation's long-term debt. Internally, both organizations were relatively compliant.

Northville was, clearly, the most besieged and factionalized organization. It was surrounded by a number of powerful stakeholders who had the power to challenge managerial decisions – the unions, action committee, Area Health Authority (AHA), Community Health Council (CHC), media, and government. Midville experienced some of these pressures, but to a lesser extent. The CHC objected to the closure, but the unions were less militant and the AHA more supportive of its management. Ville Marie was also besieged, primarily by the ministry, which dictated its funding. It also faced some internal problems with the union. Andersons also faced a duality of internal and external constraints. Internally, it was highly factionalized as a result of strong, militant unions. Externally, the U.K. operation was highly dependent on head office policies which, in turn, were being influenced by its investors and bankers, who were concerned about the company's recent performance and high level of debt, and on whom the company depended to help it in its refinancing.

This analysis shows that organizations can be categorized according to the nature and degree of their political constraints. It is important to note a number of assumptions. First, this categorization is relative. Probably, no organization is totally free of political pressures but, some clearly face far more significant pressures than others, and one would expect, therefore, to see political questions feature far more prominently in their strategies and decisions. Second, any classification must be considered dynamic: political pressures change over time and according to certain circumstances. Third, the classification may change according to the particular issue. For example, Air Canada's internal environment was relatively compliant in the context of the voluntary separation program, since the personnel affected were non-unionized managers. As regards decisions that affect unionized members, Air Canada is considerably more factionalized, particularly insofar as the International Association of Machinists and Aerospace Workers is concerned. Recent years have been characterized by a number of disputes with this and other unions. Fourth, political environments are created by managers as well as determined by circumstances. For example, the actions of managers at Northville helped exacerbate the political situation, while actions of Midville managers were designed to reduce the likelihood of a political backlash. Finally, it is worth emphasizing that, while the public agencies experienced the most significant political pressure, it was clear that private companies also had to contend with various forms of political constraints.

Political Contexts

The discussion above shows that the organizations in the sample can be classified according to the internal and external political constraints which they faced in developing retrenchment strategies. It was argued that the same analysis could be extended to other situations and

Diagram 9: Political Contexts

Internal Political Environment	*External Political Environment*: Autonomous	Besieged
Factionalized	*Internal Factions* ICI CIL	*Besieged Factions* Northville Midville Andersons Ville Marie
Compliant	*Absolute Autocracy* Whitefields	*Besieged Autocracy* Air Canada AECL

decisions, to provide a more general assessment of these organizations' political contexts. It is possible, in fact, to develop the framework to allow managers to assess the extent and nature of the political context, in which their organization has to operate (*diagram 9*).

Absolute Autocracy

Some organizations can be categorized as autonomous and compliant. They correspond to the stereotypical business enterprise which is free to conduct its business according to economic dictates. This stereotype would be a small, privately held business with a low public profile, in an unregulated industry, and with no government links or subsidies. Power is centralized in the hands of the owner – entrepreneur or senior management, and decision making is clearly top-down. Whitefields did not resemble this type of organization but was, nevertheless, characterized by a relative absence of political pressures on its retrenchment exercise, for the reasons discussed earlier.

It is important to note that we are not talking about economic, but political, constraints – an organization in this category may still face economic pressures and competition, but it does not have to accommodate a significant threat of political intervention. In reality, probably very few organizations will conform exactly to the stereotype, since most will have some political issues to contend with. It is important to note here, as has been argued in chapters 10 and 11, that managers are prone to underestimate political pressures and may place themselves in this category when they really belong elsewhere. Nevertheless, in relative terms, some organizations may approach this description and can, therefore, focus most of their attention on the economic component of strategy making.

Besieged Autocracy

Some organizations, while relatively free of internal political pressures, are besieged by external groups. Clear goals, top-down authority, and the absence of powerful internal groups enable a predominantly rational economic perspective to dominate internal decision making. External constraints, however, emanating from external stakeholders, force the organization to consider political as well economic factors when formulating external strategies.

Business organizations in regulated industries and state-owned enterprises may find themselves constrained in this way (Birnbaum, 1985; Bozeman & Straussman, 1984; Franche, 1983; Khandwalla, 1984; Zif, 1981) – and both crown corporations in the study fitted this description. There are also examples of private companies – such as the tobacco firms (see Miles & Cameron, 1982). Chrysler, following the appointment of Iaccoca, is another example. The desperate position of the company and the charismatic leadership of the new chief executive officer undoubtedly centralized power and put the onus on internal economic efficiency. The government agreement to guarantee Chrysler's loans, union concessions, and other political restrictions such as import quotas, pressure groups, and safety legislation, on the other hand, rendered the company highly dependent on a variety of external stakeholders. Chrysler's turnaround was thus the result of both economic strategies, which allowed it to regain a competitive position, and political strategies, which enabled it to negotiate time and money from its external constituencies.

Internal Factions

Some organizations have to deal with internal factions which are able to challenge the power of senior managers. In other words, the traditional top-down decision-making structure is circumvented by coalitions lower down in the organization. Adhocracies and professional bureaucracies typify this internal complexity – power is decentralized and dispersed among experts and professionals throughout the organization who, as a result, play a major role in decisions and strategy making (Mintzberg, 1979). Organizations with strong, active unions – such as CIL and ICI – also fit this classification, since the union represents a faction that can hinder managerial strategies. Finally, some organizations become, for various reasons, political arenas, in which decision making is highly politicized (Mintzberg, 1983).

Besieged Factions

Some organizations – such as the three public agencies – have to accommodate both internal and external interest groups. For example, public universities have a decentralized structure in which decision-making power is dispersed among large numbers of professors; in addition, external groups such as donors, governments, students, professional affiliations, and granting agencies are able to exert an influence on strategy formation (Hardy et al., 1983). Funding restrictions exacerbate the degree of external dependency (Hardy, 1984). Public hospitals and public adhocracies – such as the National Film Board of Canada (Mintzberg & McHugh, 1985) – also display this duality of political pressure. Private firms may face similar constraints – as the example of Andersons illustrates. Other examples might include large international engineering firms which have to reconcile the internal complexity of a matrix or project structure with the political demands of the foreign governments with which it wishes to do business.

In summary, managers can identify the nature of their political context by examining their internal and external environments. The political component of these environments is created by interest groups with the inclination and power to engage in political activity. The existence of these groups is the result of the organizational conditions discussed earlier. The organizations in the study illustrate how these conditions have manifested themselves in the context of retrenchment but, clearly, they are capable of producing political activity in many other business situations. The following section discusses the implications of these political contexts for strategy making.

Implications for Strategy Making

Organizational survival has repeatedly been linked to effective strategy making – "doing the right thing" in the face of competitive and market forces, and enabling the organization to achieve its objectives. The view of strategy embodied in this literature reflects a predominantly economic perspective (see Mintzberg, 1987). In other words, the organization is successful because it makes sensible economic decisions.

This economic perspective makes certain assumptions, including: goals are clearly defined; performance is easily measurable; rational analytic processes dominate decision making; and authority and power is centralized at the top of the organization. Only one of the four categories described above, however, conforms to these assumptions. The remaining categories have to balance economic goals with political pressures in one form or another. The existence of these political constraints has implications for the strategy-making process, which make it quite different from the traditional model. This section discusses some of these implications.

Strategy Making Will Involve a Political Analysis

If managers face besieged or factionalized contexts, they will not be able to formulate strategies with only economic factors in mind. A strategy that makes good economic sense will be of no use if, for example, powerful interest groups are able to block it. Consequently, successful managers will be assessing the political as well as the economic implications of strategy making.

> Not all the attention of the formulators is focussed on the problem and how to solve it. They must also think ahead to what is feasible ... strategic considerations are directed towards the legitimation process – building support for a proposed course of action, maintaining support held previously, deciding where compromises can be made, calculating when and where to make the strongest play and when and where to retreat, controlling information flow to advantage (Jones, 1970: 51 – 52).

Managers will, in effect, be trying to ascertain whether interest groups, with sufficient power to disrupt their decisions, exist. If indeed they do, management will have to take these groups into account when developing strategies.

Midville, particularly when compared with Northville, provides a clear example of how managers can accurately assess their political environment. Managers knew that the Community Health Council would be likely to oppose their plans, in which case the decision would be passed up to the ministerial level of government. Since the government had previously been embarrassed by hospital occupations, management knew that, in order to increase their chances of getting the closure approved, they had to reduce the chances of overt resistance. Thus, they took the necessary steps to eliminate the likelihood of opposition to the closure. Northville, on the other hand, failed to conduct any sort of political analysis, and was unaware of the potential damage that various stakeholders could inflict.

ICI also conducted a political analysis and found that, if resistance were to occur, it would probably be initiated by the shop stewards. They, therefore, involved the stewards in the rundown process. Such actions contrasted sharply with the lack of involvement of the white-collar representatives, who did not embody a similar threat and who, therefore, did not need to be involved in the same way.

Strategy Making Will Take Into Account Political Feasibility

Once it has been established that potentially dangerous interest groups exist, managers must consider ways of dealing with them. One possibility is to change and modify strategic intentions in order to accommodate them. In other words, strategic choices, according to social and political criteria, may be different to those made on purely economic grounds. The aim of these changes will be to minimize the chances of rejection (Brown, 1970; Meltsner, 1972).

> Analysis should lead to policies that can be implemented, and the study of political feasibility is one way of bridging the gap between the desirable and the possible (Meltsner, 1972: 859).

On an economic basis, Andersons would probably have closed the Scottish factory outright. It was clear, however, that presenting the unions with such a *fait accompli* would leave them with nothing to lose, and would run the risk of provoking overt opposition to the closure which, in the long term, could do more damage. The company, therefore, attempted to retain some jobs through a variety of means, in order to gain union acceptance of the closure.

Analysis and Argumentation Will Be Used Politically

If it proves impossible to modify strategy to make it more palatable to stakeholders, managers will have to try and convince them that the strategy is necessary. In which case, analysis will be carried out, not just to determine strategic options in the economic sense, but to support arguments and attack opposing positions. Similarly, information and research will be made visible to justify decisions that have already been made (Fox, 1978; Horowitz, 1970; Majone, 1977; Meltsner, 1972, Sabatier, 1978; Weiss & Bucuvalas, 1980).

> There is nothing intrinsically reprehensible in selecting the particular combination of data, facts, values and analytic methods which seems to be the most appropriate to convince a particular audience (Majone, 1976/77: 208–9).

Air Canada used the experiences of the U.S. airlines, which it incorporated into an audiovisual program to explain the need for cutbacks. Andersons tried, with limited success, to convince the unions of the need for the closure. It hampered its own efforts by refusing to release confidential figures. Both ICI and Midville convinced potential opposition groups of the need for closure by using reasons that were not strictly accurate. There were, however, highly visible and persuasive; more so, in fact, than the real reasons. Ville Marie provides an example of using analysis vis-à-vis an external party, namely the government, in an attempt to convince it to reduce budget cuts.

Strategies Will Be Negotiated

If it proves impossible to convince the relevant interest groups of the need for certain actions, it may still prove possible to negotiate with them. Coalitions may form within the organization, each advocating different positions (Stevenson et al., 1985). They may revolve around the traditional management – union dichotomy, or "management" itself may be divided into different camps. Negotiation may have to be directed at external groups (MacMillan, 1974; Murray, 1978), in which case successful managers will be those that cultivate, manipulate, and assuage the powerful actors (Khandwalla, 1984; Randall, 1973).

> Corporate plans of major strategic significance were not only "formulated" (within the company) but "negotiated" (implicitly if not explicitly) with external parties (Murray, 1978: 960).

Many of the details of the rundown process at ICI was the result of negotiation with the shop stewards. Andersons tried to negotiate, first with headquarters, to transfer a product from France to Scotland; and then with potential buyers of the factory. Eventually, through negotiations with the union, it set up Merryvale. Ville Marie tried, and failed, to negotiate with the government. Human resource managers at AECL found themselves having to negotiate with senior line executives in order to get certain options adopted.

Strategy Making May Produce Open Conflict

The actions described above – accommodation, persuasion, and negotiation – represent the unobtrusive use of power. In other words, power sources are mobilized in an attempt to *prevent* resistance from occurring (Hardy, 1985 c). If these tactics prove unsuccessful, managers will find themselves faced with overt conflict, as in the case of the factory and hospital occupations described in chapter 13. If such a situation arises, managers may only be able to carry out their strategies if they use their available power sources to defeat the oppositon that challenges them. Further discussion of such overt conflict is beyond the confines of this book. Its mention is important, however, – not to recommend its use – but to point out that it may occur, as Levie et al. (1984), for example, have found.

Strategies Will Not Be Grand Plans

In summary, when internal and external stakeholders are able to intervene, strategies will not be conceived of in splendid isolation, and put, easily and painlessly, into action. No one executive, or even group of executives, will have the power to make decisions unilaterally – information, power, authority, and responsibility will be scattered throughout the organization, or among external groups.

> When I was younger I always conceived of a room where all these [strategic] concepts were worked out for the whole company. Later I didn't find any such room. ... The strategy [of the company] may not even exist in the mind of one man (manager quoted in Quinn, 1978: 7).

Of the organizations in the study, only Whitefields formulated and implemented its retrenchment plan in anything like this manner.

Strategies Will Be Incremental and Emergent

The processes of accommodation, persuasion, negotiation, and conflict mean that strategy making will be incremental (Quinn, 1980). Formulation and implementation will not be separated into distinct phases (Narayanan & Fahey, 1982). Strategies may never be formulated because of political infeasibility; and formulated strategies may never be implemented because of political opposition or outright conflict. Thus, we can only talk about strategy as a realized phenomenon (Mintzberg, 1978; Mintzberg & Waters, 1985).

> One could argue that policies can be "good", "successful" or "rational" only *a posteriori*, to the extent that they turn out to be *adapted* to the prevailing conditions, and *adopted* by the political environment (Majone, 1976/7: 215).

Andersons' strategy was clearly incremental. The company went through a series of stages when different options were being considered and negotiated – first a transfer of production was contemplated, then a buyer for the entire factory was sought, finally another enterprise was set up. This strategy was certainly not intended when managers first considered the possibility of closing the factory. Northville's intended strategy was to close Maine Road. It was, however, never realized because it was not adapted to the prevailing political climate.

A Final Word

This final chapter has attempted to broaden the political lessons learnt from the nine organizations' experiences of retrenchment to a broader management arena. It has been argued that many different types of organization operate in political contexts; in which case organizational survival will depend upon the political skills of managers, and not just economic analyses. Despite the changes during the last twenty years in strategic planning models, ostensibly to incorporate new variables and nuances, many of the textbooks continue to adopt an economic and analytic focus. These increasingly sophisticated models have introduced new variables; the only problem is that they only tell us how to analyze them, not how to manage them (Mintzberg, 1986)

The science of planning is of limited applicability for managing political and social processes (Lyles & Lenz, 1982; Mintzberg, 1980). Failure of the economic approach is often attributed to "the nature of human beings – especially their concern about their own well being" (Abell & Hammond, 1977: 434) or resistance to change, which occurs because "reasonable people do *not* do reasonable things" (Ansoff, 1984: 388). According to the framework presented in this book, while some academics and managers may lament individual self-interest as unreasonable, it seems to be both normal and inevitable, in which case managers will have to learn how to respond to it. Moreover, more organizational concern for individual well being would appear to result in advantages for both the individual and the organization.

The problem with much of the literature is the dichotomy between prescription and description. On the one hand, we have business textbooks that provide simple, seductive models which, unfortunately, fail to apply to organizations' true dynamics. On the other hand, as we move towards the descriptive research, we often find discussions of organizations that are so "rich" that it is difficult to draw any practical conclusions. Much of the literature is, then, caught between an "analytic framework in search of realism" and "confused realism in search of an analytic framework" (Heclo, 1972: 104). Hopefully, this book will have gone some way towards "analytic realism", by using the experiences of the nine organizations to provide a pragmatic guide for managers who have to deal with the politics of survival.

Appendices

Appendix I: Glossary of Terms

Ad Tracking: service performed by personnel staff, who trace job vacancies on behalf of employees

Advance Notice: warning of job losses

Area Health Authority (AHA): administrative area in the British health service

Asset Stripping: purchase of a company where the new owners break up the company and sell off profitable parts, usually to finance the original sale

Attrition: reduction of personnel by the nonreplacement of vacant positions

Bumping: process whereby, following the removal of a job, the displaced employee moves into the job of the next most senior employee; the process is repeated until the least senior individual finally loses his or her job

Canadian Broadcast Corporation (CBC): the state-owned Canadian TV network

Closure: the shutting down of a hospital, factory, etc.

Community Health Council (CHC): organization representing patients' interests in the British health service

Cutbacks, Cuts: reduction in budgets, operations, personnel, etc.

Deadwood: term used to describe individuals who have not been productive

Decline: period during which the organization suffers from reduction in funding, revenue, profits, clients, customers, etc.

Dismissals: process whereby an individual loses his or her job; group dismissals signal that job loss is due to financial rather than individual reasons

Downsizing: reduction in size of workforce, operations, etc.; see cutbacks

Early Retirement: offer to individuals of a certain length of service to take retirement earlier than the statutory age; an incentive is usually offered and contributions to pensions etc. made up to avoid financial penalties to the individual

Enforced Dismissals/Terminations/Severance/Redundancies/Layoffs: group dismissals in which the individuals are selected by the management and have no choice about whether to leave or not

Full Employment: refers here to Whitefields' practice of not laying off employees

Globe & Mail: Canadian newspaper

Job Security: see Full Employment

Job Shop: room at ICI in which job vacancies were posted

Lay member: member of a board or committee, etc. who has no technical knowledge, usually appointed to represent the public interest

Layoffs: job losses due to financial reasons; such individuals are laid off; can be voluntary or enforced

National Health Service (NHS): the British health service

Occupation: actions by employees where the factory or hospital is physically occupied to prevent the sale of assets; in the NHS it has involved the continuation of services by doctors, nurses, and other employees to keep the hospital functioning after the scheduled closure. Factory occupations were relatively common in the U.K. during the early 1970s; a number of hospital occupations occurred during the middle to late 1970s

Outplacement: activities designed to help employees who lose their jobs find new employment

Placement: see Outplacement

Plant: factory

Rationalization: reduction of operations, manufacturing sites, services, etc.

Redeployment: see Outplacement

Redundancies: see Layoffs

Redundancy Compensation: payment to employees who lose their jobs for financial reasons; required by law in Canada and U.K.

Relocation: moving of either a factory to a new location or of an employee to a new job

Reorganization (of the NHS): the structure introduced in the NHS in 1974. Midville and Northville were operating under this structure at the time of the research; it has since changed

Retrenchment: reduction in scale or scope of activities; may involve cutbacks, rationalization, closures, layoffs, etc.

Rundown: time during which operations at a factory are reduced prior to actual closure

Severance: see Layoff

Severance Terms: see Redundancy Compensation

Shop Steward: union official

Stakeholder: interest group with a stake in the organization; in this case with a stake in the retrenchment program and its outcome

Termination: see Dismissal

Trusteeship: process whereby board of a public agency is replaced by government appointees; usually occurs when the board in question has failed to meet government regulations

Turnaround: process whereby a declining organization is restored to health

Unemployment Insurance Contribution (UIC): government payment to unemployed individuals

Voluntary Dismissals/Terminations/Severance/Redundancies/Layoffs: refers to the situation where individuals can choose whether to leave the organization

Works: factory

Appendix II: Abbreviations

AHA:	Area Health Authority (Midville, Northville)
AMT:	Area Management Team (Midville, Northville)
APEX:	Association of Professional, Executive, Chemical, and Computer Staff (ICI)
ASTM:	Association of Scientific, Technical, and Managerial Staff (ICI)
ATO:	Area Team of Officers (Midville, Northville)
AUEW:	Amalgamated Union of Engineering Workers (ICI, Andersons)
CALEA:	Canadian Airline Employees Association (Air Canada)
CALFAA:	Canadian Airline Flight Attendants Association (Air Canada)
CALPA:	Canadian Airline Pilots Association (Air Canada)
CEO:	Chief Executive Officer (Air Canada)
CHC:	Community Health Council (Midville, Northville)
CSS:	cap sensitive slurry explosives production (CIL)
DGH:	District General Hospital (Midville, Northville)
DHSS:	Department of Health and Social Security (Midville, Northville)
DMT:	District Management Team (Midville, Northville)
EETPU:	Electrical, Electronic, Telecommunications, and Plumbing Union (ICI)
ERC:	Employee Relations Committee (Ville Marie)
ERP:	Early Retirement Program (Whitefields)
GP:	General Practitioner (Midville, Northville)
HOD:	Head of Department (ICI)
HR:	Human Resources (Air Canada)
HRD:	Human Resource Department (AECL)
HRG:	Human Resource Group (CIL)
IAMAW:	International Association of Machinists and Aerospace Workers (Air Canada)
JMAC:	Joint Manpower Adjustment Committee (AECL)
JPC:	Joint Planning Committee (AECL)
JUCC:	Joint Union Coordinating Committee (Andersons)
LEP:	Least Essential Position (Air Canada)
MAS:	Ministère des Affaires Sociales (Ville Marie)
MP:	Member of Parliament (Andersons, Midville, Northville)
MSC:	Manpower Steering Committee (AECL)
NG:	nitroglycerine-based explosives (CIL)
NHS:	National Health Service (Midville, Northville)

NUGMU:	National Union of General and Municipal Workers (ICI)
NUM:	National Union of Miners
NUPE:	National Union of Public Employees (Northville)
PSAC:	Public Service Alliance (AECL)
RAWP:	Resource Allocation Working Party (Midville, Northville)
RHA:	Regional Health Authority (Midville, Northville)
RSG:	Redeployment Steering Group (ICI)
SPEA:	Society of Professional Engineers and Associates (AECL)
STUC:	Scottish Trades Union Congress (Andersons)
TASS:	Technical, Administrative and Supervisory Section of the AUEW (Andersons)
TUC:	Trades Union Congress (Andersons)
UCATT:	Union of Construction, Allied Trades, and Technicians (ICI)
USWA:	United Steel Workers of America (CIL)
UCS:	Upper Clyde Shipbuilders
UIC:	Unemployment Insurance Contribution (Air Canada)
VSP:	Voluntary Separation Program (Air Canada)

Appendix III: Details of Company Provisions

ICI

January 1975	Company's statement on job security
March 1975	Closure of Mountside in five- to ten-years forecast
Mid-1975	Working parties established (reported late 1975)
December 1985	Appointment of Redeployment Manager
	Divisional board accepts closure plan
March 1976	Announcement of closure plan
	Policy statement on availability of severance terms
April 1976	Meeting with staff unions
June 1976	Meeting with manual unions
September 1976	Establishment of manual RSG
	Opening of "job shop"
November 1976	Meeting with manual unions (who agree to closure)
February 1977	Policy statement on retraining as an aid to redeployment
December 1977	2-day pre-retirement course for staff
April 1978	RSG for staff groups established
1980	Last sheds close

CIL

June 7, 1983	Announcement of closure
June 7–15, 1983	All employees scheduled to see one of four counsellors brought in from head office

June 14, 1983	Advisement of placement committees
June 16–21, 1983	Personnel superintendent from CIL York works available on site to discuss questions (30 individuals attended)
June 22–24, 1983	Two external consultants hired to provide group counselling on financial planning and/or retirement (all 123 employees affected attended)
June 27, 1983	Canada Employment Centre (CEC) enrolled employees in their job search program (91 employees registered for this program)
June 28, 1983	CEC provided a one hour general information session (82 employees attended)
July 6, 1983	The two external consultants returned for individual sessions (24 participated in retirement sessions, 45 participated in financial sessions)
July 13, 1983	Personnel officers from CIL York works were on site to interview employees for possible employment (27 people were interviewed but no vacancies developed)
July 20, 1983	Personnel officers from CIL Brampton works interviewed 26 employees (7 employees subsequently accepted offers of employment)
August 1983	Seminars were arranged with CEC on job search techniques (32 participated)
September 1983	All retiring/redundant individuals were interviewed by the personnel superintendent, and the different ways of receiving relocation allowances, pension refunds, and vacation monies were discussed

AECL

November 1982	Group and individual notices of closure
	Termination compensation and special indemnity: 2 weeks' pay for the first and 1 week's pay

	for each additional year of service plus 1/2 (or 1) day's pay while under age 45 (or over 45) – minimum of 8 days, maximum of 25 (or 50 days)
	General information sessions
	"Job search techniques" seminar run by Thorne, Stevenson, & Kellog
December 1982/ January 1983	"Interviewing techniques" seminar
	Assistance with resume preparation
	JMACs and JPC established
	Exploratory letters sent out to external employers; follow-up telephone calls; liaison; outplacement notices placed in publications
	Special efforts to relocate redundant employees to other AECL sites
	Personal counselling
	Outplacement centre established
February 1983	Job fair
	Personal benefits summary given to employees
	Time away from work supported for job interviews, job fairs, outplacement centre visits, committee meetings, etc.
	Employees who found employment and left early were not penalized on severance pay

Appendix IV: Membership and Terms of Reference of JMACs and JPC

The Joint Planning Committee (JPC) consisted of 1 Labour Canada observer, 8 company representatives, and 2 representatives and 2 alternates from each of the following: SPEA; PSAC; and non-unionized technicians; the non-unionized clerical, secretarial, and administrative support staff. JMACs were established for SPEA, PSAC, the technical group, and the administrative group, each with around 20 members including company representatives, employee representatives and alternates, an independent chairman, and a representative from the Canada Employment and Immigration Commission.

The terms of reference were as follows for the non-unionized Joint Manpower Adjustment Committees (JMACs):

(a) To develop an orderly program of adjustment, which will alleviate to the extent possible the problems which will result from the company's decision to reduce its level of manpower in line with operational requirements.

(b) To recommend to the company any courses of action which the Committee deems to be essential to the development of an effective manpower adjustment program.

(c) With the assistance of the Manpower Consultative Service and the Provincial Minister to bring to bear and make the most effective use of all public manpower measures and services available from the Federal and Provincial Governments.

(d) Establish a JMAC Grievance Subcommittee to address any grievances which emanate from the layoff. This Subcommittee will meet as often as necessary and report to the main JMAC.

(e) Establish a JMAC Outplacement Subcommittee to explore and implement procedures to assist the laid-off employees in their search for alternate employment. This Subcommittee will meet as often as necessary and report to the main JMAC.

The terms of reference were as follows for the unionized Joint Manpower Adjustment Committees (JMACs):

(a) To develop an orderly program of adjustment, which will alleviate to the extent possible the problems which will result from the company's decision to reduce its level of manpower in line with operational requirements.

(b) To recommend to the company and the union a joint course of action which the Committee deems to be essential in the development of an effective manpower adjustment program.

(c) With the assistance of the Manpower Consultative Service and the Provincial Minister to bring to bear and make the most effective use of all public manpower measures and services available from the Federal and Provincial Governments.

(d) With the assistance of the Manpower Consultative Service to appoint a suitable person to act as chairman.

Appendix V: Methodology

This research was conducted by means of in-depth, semi-structured interviews with members of the relevant interest groups, as listed below.

ICI: 38 interviews were conducted with corporate and local managers; employees; ex-employees; union representatives; and union officials.

CIL: 25 interviews were conducted with divisional and corporate managers; members of the human resources division; and ex-employees.

Whitefields: 12 interviews were conducted with representatives of the human resource department.

Andersons: 27 interviews were conducted with senior and local managers; union representatives; union officials; employees; ex-employees.

AECL: 26 interviews were conducted with senior managers; members of human resources; union representatives; employees, and ex-employees.

Air Canada: 15 interviews were conducted with executives; human resource managers; and employees.

Ville Marie: 35 interviews were conducted with central and local managers; employees; ex-employees; union representatives; and board members.

Midville: 16 interviews were conducted with area and district managers; employees; ex-employees; union representatives; and representatives of the CHC and AHA.

Northville: 27 interviews were conducted with area and district managers; employees; ex-employees; union representatives; and representatives of the CHC and AHA.

These interviews were recorded and lasted between one and three hours. In all cases, except Whitefields, I was allowed to interview anyone I chose. In the case of Whitefields, I was restricted to members of human resources. The number of interviews was determined by time and access. In general, the aim was to speak to representatives of all the interest groups participating in and affected by the retrenchment program, particularly "active" individuals who had played a key role in events as well as a selection of "passive" individuals who had been affected by these events. Interviewing in the U.K. took place between 1978 and 1981; interviewing in Canada occurred between 1983 and 1985. In addition, an analysis was made of documentary evidence – both published and unpublished. Documentation included annual reports, newspapers articles, etc., as well as internal reports, memoranda, and correspondence, which was made available by all parties.

References

Abell, D. F. & Hammond, J. S., *Strategic Market Planning*, Englewood Cliffs, N. J.: Prentice-Hall, 1979.

Aharoni, Y., *The Foreign Investment Decision Process*, Cambridge, Mass.: Harvard University Press, 1966.

Angle, H. L., Manz, C. C. & Van de Ven, A. H., 'Integrating Human Resource Management and Corporate Strategy: A Preview of the 3M Story', *Human Resource Management*, 24(1), 51–68, 1985.

Ansoff, H. I., *Implanting Strategic Management*, Englewood Cliffs, N. J.: Prentice-Hall, 1984.

Astley, W. G. & Fombrun, C. J., 'Collective Strategy: Social Ecology of Organizational Environments', *Academy of Management Review*, 8(4), 576–587, 1983.

Astley, W. G., Axelsson, R., Butler, R. J., Hickson, D. J. & Wilson, D. C., 'Complexity and Cleavage: Dual Explanations of Strategic Decision-Making', *Journal of Management Studies*, 19(4), 357–375, 1982.

Baird, L., Meshoulam, I. & DeGive, G., 'Meshing Human Resources Planning with Strategic Business Planning: A Model Approach', *Personnel*, 50, (5), 14–25, 1983.

Baker, R. J. S., 'Organization Theory and the Public Sector', *Journal of Management Studies*, 6, 15–32, 1969.

Baker, R. J. S., *Administrative Theory and Public Administration*, London: Hutchison, 1972.

Ball, R., 'Taming Britain's Unions', *Fortune*, 109(8), 134–142, April 16, 1984.

Barnard, K., *NHS Reorganization: Issues and Prospects*, Leeds, England: Nuffield Centre for Health Service Studies, 1974.

Batt, W. L., 'Canada's Good Example with Displaced Workers', *Harvard Business Review*, 61(4), 6–22, 1983.

Behn, R. D., 'Closing the Massachusetts Public Training Schools', *Policy Science*, 7, 151–171, 1976.

Behn, R. D., 'How to Terminate a Public Policy', *Policy Analysis*, 4, 393–413, 1978.

Behn, R. D., 'Leadership for Cutback Management: The Use of Corporate Strategy', *Public Administration Review*, 40(6), 613–620, 1980.

Benson, J., 'Trade Union Attitudes to Job Sharing in Australia and Some Lessons for the U.K.', *Industrial Relations Journal*, 13(3), 13–20, 1982.

Berger, L. A. & Glass, H. E., 'Linking Business and Human Resource Strategy', *Planning Review*, 11(6), 26–29, 1983.

Beynon, H., *Working for Ford*, London: Allen Lane, 1973.

Beynon, H. & Wainwright, H., *The Workers' Report on Vickers*, London: Pluto Press, 1973.

Bilbeault, D. B., *Corporate Turnaround*, New York: McGraw-Hill, 1982.

Birnbaum, P. H., 'Political Strategies of Regulated Organizations as Functions of Context and Fear', *Strategic Management Journal*, 6(2), 135–150, 1985.

Blyton, P., 'The Industrial Relations of Work Sharing', *Industrial Relations Journal*, 13(3), 6–13, 1982.

Bolle, M. J., *Overview of Plant Closing and Industrial Migration Issues in the U.S.*, Washington: Library of Congress, 1980.

Bower, J. L., 'Effective Public Management', *Harvard Business Review*, 55(2), 131–140, 1977.

Bozeman, B., & Straussman, J. D. 'Publicness and Resource Management Strategies', in R. H. Hall & R. G. Quinn (eds.), *Organizational Theory and Public Policy*, Beverly Hills: Sage, 1984.

Bradley, K., *Worker Control as a State Managerial Device: A Study of the Scottish Daily News'*, Ph. D. Thesis, University of Essex, UK, 1978.

Brewer, G., 'Termination: Hard Choices – Harder Questions', *Public Administration Review*, 38(4), 38–344, 1978.

Bright, D., Sawbridge, D. & Rees, B., 'Industrial Relations of Recession', *Industrial Relations Journal*, 14(3), 24–33, 1983.

Brown, R. G. S., *The Administrative Process in Britain*, London: Methuen, 1970.

Bryer, R. A., Brignall, T. J. & Maunders, A. R., *Accounting for BSC*, Aldershot, England: Gower Press, 1982.

Buchan, A., *The Right to Work*, London: Calder & Boyars, 1972.

Burke, R. J., Cunliffe, A., Wolpin, J. & DuWors, R. E., 'Trainee Experiences in Industrial Retraining Programs', Unpublished paper, 1983.

Buss, T. F. & Redburn, F. S., *Shutdown at Youngstown: Public Policy for Mass Unemployment*, New York: State University of New York Press, 1983.

Cameron, K., 'Strategic Responses to Conditions of Decline: Higher Education and the Private Sector', *Journal of Higher Education*, 54, 359–380, 1983.

Cameron, K. & Zammuto, R., 'Matching Managerial Strategies to Conditions of Decline', *Human Resource Management*, 22(4), 359–376, 1983.

Carrothers, A. W. R. Munro, J. J., & Perrault, C. H., *Report of the Commission of Inquiry into Redundancies and Lay-offs*, Ottawa: Labour Canada, 1979.

Carter, E. E., *A Behavioral Approach to Firm Investment*, Ph. D. Thesis, Carnegie–Mellon University, Pittburgh, 1969.

Child, J., 'Organizational Structure, Environment and Performance: The Role of Strategic Choice', *Sociology*, 6, 1–22, 1972.

Clarke, T., 'Redundancy, Worker Resistance and the Community', in G. Craig, M. Mayo, & N. Sharman, (eds.), *Jobs and Community Action*, London: Routledge & Kegan Paul, 1979.

Cooke, S., 'ICI's Jolly Captain', *Business Week*, June 3, 62–63, 1987.

Crozier, M., *The Bureaucratic Phenomenon*, Chicago: Chicago University Press, 1964.

Cyert, R. & March, J.G., *A Behavioural Theory of the Firm*, New York: Wiley, 1963.

Dean, M., 'Why the Ministry has Switched Back to the Smaller Hospitals', *Guardian*, 4 June, p. 17, 1980.

Dowling, J. & Pfeffer, J., 'Organizational Legitimacy: Social Values and Organizational Behaviour', *Pacific Sociological Review*, 18(1), 122–135, 1975.

Dror, Yehezkel, 'Policy Analysts: A New Professional Role in Government Service', *Public Administration Review*, 27, 197–203, 1967.

Dyer, L., 'Bringing Human Resources into the Strategy Formulation Process', *Human Resource Management*, 22(4), 257–271, 1983.

Edwards, P., 'Britain's Changing Strike Problem', *Industrial Relations Journal*, 13(2), 46–68, 1982.

Eleen, John & Ashley, B., *Shutdown: The Impact of Plant Shutdown, Extensive Employment Termination and Layoffs on the Workers and the Community*, Toronto: Federation of Labour, 1971.

Ellig, B., 'Pay Policies While Downsizing the Organization: A Systematic Approach', *Personnel*, 60(3), 26–35, 1983.

Eves, J.H., 'When a Plant Shuts Down: Easing the Pain', *Personnel*, 62(2), 16–23, 1985.

Fahey, Liam, 'On Strategic Management Decision Processes', *Strategic Management Journal*, 2, 43–60, 1981.

Ferris, R., Schellenberg, D.A. & Zammuto, R.F., 'Human Resource Management Strategies in Declining Industries', *Human Resource Management*, 23(4), 381–394, 1984.

Foltman, F., *White and Blue Collars In a Mill Shutdown*, New York: Cornell University, 1968.

Fox, A., 'Industrial Relations: A Social Critique of Pluralist Ideology', in J. Child (ed.), *Man and Organization*, London: Allen & Unwin, 1973.

Fox, P.D., *By Guess or By What: Information Without Design in the NHS*, Oxford: Oxford University Press, 1978.

Franche, P., 'A Case for Crown Corporations', Remarks to Colloque ENAP-83, École nationale d'administration publique, September 30, 1983.

Fryer, R.H., 'Redundancy Values and Public Policy', *Industrial Relations Journal*, 4(2), 2–19, 1973.

Fuller, R., Jordan, C. & Anderson, R., 'Retrenchment: Lay-Off Procedures in a Non-Profit Organization', *Personnel*, 59, 17–24, 1982.

Galosy, J. R., 'Meshing Human Resources Planning with Strategic Business Planning: One Company's Experience', *Personnel*, 60(5), 26–35, 1983.

Garrett, J., *The Management of Government*, Harmondsworth: Pelican, 1972.

Gawthrop, L. C., *Administrative Politics and Social Change*, New York: St. Martins, 1971.

Glassberg, A. D., 'Organizational Responses to Municipal Budget Decreases', *Public Administration Review*, 38(4), 325–332, 1978.

Gordus, J. P., Jarley, P. & Ferman, L. A., *Plant Closings and Economic Dislocation*, Kalamazoo, Mich.: W. E. Upjohn Institute for Employment Research, 1981.

Gospel, H. & Littler, C., *Managerial Strategies and Industrial Relations*, London: Heineman, 1982.

Gravitz, D., 'Opening the Early Retirement Window', *Personnel*, 60(2), 53–57, 1983.

Greenhalgh, L., 'Managing the Job Insecurity Crisis', *Human Resource Management*, 22(4), 431–444, 1983.

Greenwood, J., *Worker Sit-ins and Job Protection*, Aldershot, England: Gower Press, 1977.

Greenwood, R., Hinings, C. R. & Ranson, S., 'The Politics of the Budgetary Process in English Local Government', *Political Studies*, 25(1), 25–47, 1976.

Hambrick, D. C. & Schecter, S. M., 'Turnaround Strategies for Mature Industrial-Product Business Units', *Academy of Management Review*, 26(2), 231–248, 1983.

Hammerman, H., 'Five Case Studies of Displaced Workers', *Monthly Labour Review*, 87(6), 663–670, 1964.

Hardy, C., 'The Management of University Cutbacks: Politics, Planning and Participation', *Canadian Journal of Higher Education*, 14(1), 80–89, 1984.

Hardy, C., *Managing Organisational Closure*, Aldershot, England: Gower Press, 1985 a.

Hardy, C., 'Responses to Organizational Closure: Patterns of Resistance and Quiescence', *Industrial Relations Journal*, 16(1), 16–24, 1985 b.

Hardy, C., 'The Nature of Unobtrusive Power', *Journal of Management Studies*, 22(4), 384–399, 1985 c.

Hardy, C., 'Resisting Cutbacks: Some Issues for Public Sector Administrators', *Canadian Public Administration*, 18(4), 531–549, 1985 d.

Hardy, C., 'Strategies for Retrenchment: Reconciling Individual and Organizational Needs', *Canadian Journal of Administrative Sciences*, 3(2), 275–289, 1986 a.

Hardy, C., 'Effective Retrenchment: Human Resource Implications', *Journal of General Management*, 12(3), 76–92, 1986 b.

Hardy, C., 'Management in the National Health Service: Using Politics Effectively', *Public Policy and Administration*, 1(1), 1–17, 1986 c.

Hardy, C., 'Investing in Retrenchment: Avoiding the Hidden Costs', *California Management Review*, 29, 111–125, 1987 a.

Hardy, C., 'Turnaround Strategies in Universities', *Planning for Higher Education*, 16(1), 9–23, 1987 b.

Hardy, C. & Pettigrew, A. M., 'The Use of Power in Managerial Strategies for Change', in R. S. Rosenbloom (ed.), *Research on Technological Innovation, Management and Policy*, 2, 11–45, 1985.

Hardy, C., Langley, A., Mintzberg, H. & Rose, J., 'Strategy Formation in the University Setting', *Review of Higher Education*, 6(4), 407–433, 1983.

Harmon, M. M., 'Administrative Policy Formulation and the Public Interest', *Public Administration Review*, 29, 483–491, 1969.

Harrison, B., 'Plant Closures: Efforts to Cushion the Blow', *Monthly Labour Review*, 197(6), 41–43, 1984.

Haywood, S. C., 'The Politics of Management in Health Care: A British Perspective', *Journal of Health Politics, Policy and Law*, 8(3), 424–443, 1983.

Heclo, H. H., 'Review Article: Policy Analysis', *British Journal of Political Science*, 2, 83–108, 1972.

Heclo, H. H. & Wildavsky, A., *The Private Government of Public Money*, London: Macmillan, 1974.

Hemmingway, J. & Keyser, W., *Who's in Charge?*, Oxford: Metra, 1975.

Hercus, T. F., 'Human Resource Planning during Periods of Budget Constraint', *Canadian Personnel and Industrial Relations Journal*, 25(4), 35–38, 1978.

Hickson, D. J., Butler, R. J., Cray, D., Mallory, G. R. & Wilson, D., *Top Decisions*, San Francisco: Jossey Bass, 1986.

Hinings, C. R. & Greenwood, R., 'Research into Local Government Organization', *Public Administration Bulletin*, 15, 21–30, 1973.

Hofer, C. W., 'Turnaround Strategies', *Journal of Business Strategy*, 1, 19–31, 1980.

Horowitz, I. L., 'Social Science Mandarins: Policymaking as a Political Formula', *Policy Sciences*, 1, 339–360, 1970.

Huff, A. S., 'Organizations as Political Systems: Implications for Diagnosis, Change, and Stability", in T. G. Cummings (ed.), *Systems Theory for Organization Development*, London: Wiley, 1980.

Huitt, R., 'Political Feasibility', in I. Sharkansky (ed.), *Policy Analysis in Political Science*, Chicago: Markham, 1970.

Hunter, D. J., *Coping with Uncertainty*, Chichester, England: Research Studies Press, 1980.

Hyman, R. & Fryer, R. H., 'Trade Unions – Sociological and Political Economy' in J. B. McKinlay (ed.), *Processing People*, London: Holt, Rinehart & Winston, 1975.

Jain, H. & Murray, V., 'Why the Human Resources Management Function Fails', *California Management Review*, 26(4), 95–110, 1984.

Jick, T. D. & Murray, V. V., 'The Management of Hard Times: Budget Cutbacks in Public Sector Organizations', *Organization Studies*, 3, 141–169, 1982.

Jones, C. O., *An Introduction to the Study of Public Policy*, Belmont, Cal.: Wadsworth, 1970.

Kanter, R. M., *The Change Masters: Innovation for Productivity in the American Corporation*, New York: Simon and Schuster, 1983.

Keeling, D., *Management in Government*, London: Allen & Unwin, 1972.

Keim, G. D. & Zeithaml, C. P., 'Corporate Strategy and Legislative Decision Making: A Review and Contingency Approach', *Academy of Management Review*, 11(4), 828–843, 1986.

Keim, G. D., Zeithaml, C. P. & Baysinger, B. D., 'New Directions for Corporate Public Strategy', *Sloan Management Review*, 25(3), 53–61, 1984.

Khandwalla, P. N., 'Some Lessons for the Management of Public Enterprises', *International Studies of Management & Organization*, 14(2–3), 167–196, 1984.

King, P. F., *An Investigation of the Process of Large-Scale Capital Investments: Decision-Making in Diversified Hierarchical Organizations*, Ph. D. thesis, University of London, 1976.

Kochan, T. A., McKersie, R. B. & Cappelli, P., 'Strategic Choice and Industrial Relations Theory', *Industrial Relations*, 23(1), 16–39, 1984.

Lambright, W. H. & Sapolsky, H. M., 'Terminating Federal Research and Development Programs', *Policy Sciences*, 7, 183–197, 1976.

Lehr, R. I. & Middlebrooks, D. J., 'Work Force Reduction', *Personnel Journal*, 63(10), 50–54, 1984.

Levie, H., Gregory, D., & Lorentzen, L. (eds.), *Fighting Closures: Deindustrialization and the Trade Unions 1979–1983*, Nottingham, England: Spokesman, 1984.

Levine, C. H., 'Organizational Decline and Cutback Management', *Public Administrative Review*, 38(4), 316–325, 1978.

Levine, C. H., 'More on Cutback Management: Hard Questions for Hard Times', *Public Administrative Review*, 39(2), 179–183, 1979.

Levine, C. H., Rubin, I. S. & Wolohojian, G. G., *The Politics of Retrenchment*, Beverly Hills, Cal.: Sage, 1981.

Levine, H. Z., 'Corporate Responsibilities during Layoffs', *Personnel*, 60(4), 55–58, 1983.

Luce, S., *Retrenchment and Beyond*, Ottawa: Conference Board of Canada, 1983.

Lyles, M. A. & Lenz, R. T., 'Managing the Planning Process: A Field Study of the Human Side of Planning', *Strategic Management Journal*, 3(2), 105–118, 1982.

MacMillan, I. C., 'Business Strategies for Political Action', *Journal of General Management*, 2(1), 51–63, 1974.

MacMillan, I. C., *Strategy Formulation: Political Concepts*, New York: West, 1978.

MacMillan, I. C. & Schuler, R. S., 'Gaining a Competitive Edge Through Human Resources', *Personnel*, 62(4), 24–29, 1985.

Majone, C., 'The Uses of Policy Analysis', in *The Future and the Past: Essays on Programs*, New York: Russell Sage Foundation, 1977.

McNeff, N., McNeff, M., O'Connell, J. & O'Connell, G., 'Alternatives to Employee Lay-offs: Work-Sharing and Pre-Layoff Consultation', *Personnel*, 55(1), 60–64, 1978.

McQueen, J., 'Integrating Human Resource Planning with Strategic Planning', *Canadian Public Administration*, 27(1), 1–13, 1983.

Meltsner, A. J., 'Political Feasibility and Policy Analysis', *Public Administration Review*, 32, 859–867, 1972.

Meltz, N., Reid, F. & Swart, G., *Sharing the Work – An Analysis of the Issues in Worksharing and Jobsharing*, Toronto: University of Toronto Press, 1981.

Meyer, J. W. & Rowan, B., 'Formal Structure as Myth and Ceremony', *American Journal of Sociology*, 83(2), 340–363, 1977/8.

Meyerson, M. & Bamfield, E. C., *Politics, Planning, and the Public Interest*, New York: The Free Press, 1955.

Miles, R. H. & Cameron, K. S., *Coffin Nails and Corporate Strategies*, Englewood Cliffs, N. J.: Prentice-Hall, 1982.

Miles, R. T. & Snow, C. L., 'Designing Strategic Human Resources Systems', *Organizational Dynamics*, 13, 36–52, 1984.

Mintzberg, H., 'Patterns in Strategy Formation', *Management Science*, 24(9), 934–948, 1978.

Mintzberg, H., *The Structuring of Organizations*, Englewood Cliffs, N. J.: Prentice-Hall, 1979.

Mintzberg, H., 'Beyond Implementation: An Analysis of the Resistance to Policy Analysis', *Infor*, 18(2), 100–138, 1980.

Mintzberg, H., *Power In and Around Organizations*, Englewood Cliffs, N. J.: Prentice-Hall, 1983.

Mintzberg, H., 'Power and Organization Life Cycles', *The Academy of Management Review*, 9(2), 207–224, 1984 a.

Mintzberg, H., 'Who Should Control the Corporation?', *California Management Review*, 27(1), 90–115, 1984 b.

Mintzberg, H., *The Planning School: Strategy Formation as a Formal Process*, unpublished manuscript, 1986.

Mintzberg, H., 'The Strategy Concept I: Five Ps for Strategy', *California Management Review*, 30(1), 11–24, 1987.

Mintzberg, H. & Jorgensen, J., 'Emergent Strategy for Public Policy', *Canadian Public Administration*, 30(2), 214–229, 1987.

Mintzberg, H. & McHugh, A., 'Strategy Formation in an Adhocracy', *Administrative Science Quarterly*, 30, 160–197, 1985.

Mintzberg, H. & Waters, J. A., 'Of Strategies, Deliberate and Emergent', *Strategic Management Journal*, 6, 257–272, 1985.

Monthly Labour Review, 'Progress Report of Armour's Tripartite Automation Committee', 84(8), 851–857, 1961.

Morin, W. J. & Yorks, L., *Outplacement Techniques*, New York: AMACOM 1982.

Mumford, E. & Pettigrew, A. M., *Implementing Strategic Decisions*, London: Longman, 1975.

Murray, E. A., 'Strategic Choice as a Negotiated Outcome', *Management Science*, 24(9), 960–972, 1978.

Narayanan, V. K. & Fahey, L., 'The Micro Politics of Strategy Formulation', *Academy of Management Review*, 7(1), 25–34, 1982.

Perigoe, J. Rae, 'Company Help for the Laid-Off', *Canadian Personnel and Industrial Relations Journal*, 17(6), 40–42, 1980.

Pettigrew, A. M., *The Politics of Organizational Decision-Making*, London: Tavistock, 1973.

Pettigrew, A. M., 'Conference Review: Issues of Change', in P. Warr, (ed.), *Personal Goals and Work Design*, London: Wiley, 1976.

Pettigrew, A. M., 'Strategy Formulation as a Political Process', *International Studies of Management and Organizations*, 7(2), 78–87, 1977.

Pettigrew, A. M., *The Awakening Giant: Continuity and Change in ICI*, Oxford: Basil Blackwell, 1985.

Pfeffer, J., *Power in Organizations*, Marshfield, Mass.: Pitman, 1981.

Pfeffer, J. & Salancik, G. R., *The External Control of Organizations*, New York: Harper & Row, 1978.

Portis, B. & Suys, M., *A Study of the Closing of the Kelvinator Plant in London, Ontario*, London, Ontario: University of Western Ontario, 1970.

Price, R. & Bain, G. S., 'Union Growth in Britain: Retrospect and Prospect', *British Journal of Industrial Relations*, 21(1), 46–68, 1983.

Price, R. H. & D'Aunno, T., 'Managing Work Force Reduction', *Human Resource Management*, 22(4), 431–444, 1983.

Purcell, J., *Good Industrial Relations: Theory and Practice*, London: Macmillan, 1981.

Purcell, J., 'The Management of Industrial Relations in the Modern Corporation: Agenda for Research', *British Journal of Industrial Relations*, 21, 1–16, 1983.

Quinn, J. B., 'Strategic Change: "Logical Incrementalism"', *Sloan Management Review*, 19, 7–21, 1978.

Quinn, J. B., 'Managing Strategic Change', *Sloan Management Review*, 21(4), 3–20, 1980.

Rainey, H. G., 'Organization Theory and Political Science: Organizational Typologies, Political Variables, and Policy Studies', *Policy Studies*, 13(1), 5–22, 1984.

Rainey, H. G., Backoff, R. W. & Levine, C. H., 'Comparing Public and Private Organizations', *Public Administration Review*, 36, 233–244, 1976.

Randall, R., 'Influence of Environmental Support and Policy Space on Organizational Behaviour', *Administrative Science Quarterly*, 18, 236–247, 1973.

Reuber, G., 'Better Bureaucracies', *Policy Options*, 3(5), 11–14, 1982.

Ruben, George, 'Economy Improves, Bargaining Problems Persist in 1983', *Monthly Labor Review*, 107(1), 33–43, 1984.

Sabatier, P., 'The Acquisitional Utilization of Technical Information by Administrative Agencies', *Administrative Science Quarterly*, 23, 396–417, 1978.

Sadlier-Brown, P., *Work-Sharing in Canada: Problems and Possibilities*, Montreal: C. D. Howe Research Institute, 1978.

Schendel, D. G. & Hofer, W. C. (eds.), *Strategic Management: A New View of Business Policy and Planning*, Boston: Little, Brown & Co, 1979.

Schendel, D. G. & Patton, G. R., 'Corporate Stagnation and Turnover', *Journal of Economics and Business*, 28(3), 236–241, 1976.

Schendel, D. G., Patton, G. R. & Riggs, J., 'Corporate Turnaround Strategies: A Study of Profit Decline & Recovery', *Journal of General Management*, 3(3), 3–11, 1976.

Sexton, J., *Blue Collar Workers Displaced by Complete and Permanent Plant Shutdowns: The Quebec Experience*, Laval: Université Laval, 1974.

Shultz, G. P. & Weber, A. R., *Strategies for the Displaced Worker*, New York: Harper and Row, 1966.

Simon, H. A., 'A Behavioral Model of Rational Choice', *Quarterly Journal of Economics*, 69(1), 493–513, 1955.

Sisson, K., *The Management of Collective Bargaining: An International Comparison*, Oxford: Blackwell, 1983.

Slater, H. W., 'Medium Term Prospects for the UK Economy', *Journal of General Management*, 10(2), 4–18, 1984.

Smith Ring, P. & Perry, J. L., 'Strategic Management in Public Organizations: Implications of Distinctive Contexts and Constraints', *Academy of Management Review*, 10(2), 276–286, 1985.

Soskice, D., 'Industrial Relations and the British Economy', *Industrial Relations*, 23(3), 306–322, 1984.

Stern, J., 'Adjustment to Plant Closure', *Monthly Labour Review*, 90(1), 42–46, 1969.

Stevenson, W. B., Pearce, J. L., & Porter, L. W., 'The Concept of "Coalition" in Organization Theory and Research', *Academy of Management Review*, 10(2), 256–268, 1985.

Stybel, L. J., *Managing Human Resource Termination: The Interpersonal Conduct and Organizational Consequences of Executive Dismissal*, D. Ed thesis, Harvard University, Cambridge, 1978.

Sutton, R. I., 'Managing Organizational Death', *Human Resource Management*, 22(4), 390–412, 1983.

Sutton, R. I., Eisenhardt, K. M. & Jucker, J. V., 'Managing Organizational Decline: Lessons from Atari', *Organization Dynamics*, 14(4), 17–29, 1986.

Ukeles, J. B., 'Policy Analysis: Myth or Reality?', *Public Administration Review*, 37, 223–228, 1977.

Ullman, J., 'Helping Workers Locate Jobs Following a Plant Shutdown', *Monthly Labour Review*, 92(4), 35–40, 1969.

Unwin, H. & Murray, G., 'Democracy and Trade Unions', *Industrial Relations Journal*, 14(4), 21–30, 1983.

Ursell, G. D. M., *A Sociological Study of the Containment of an Extra-Union Organization amongst Steel Workers*, MSc thesis, Bradford, UK, 1976.

Vickers, G., *The Art of Judgement*, New York: Basic Books, 1965.

Walsh, K., Hinings, R., Greenwood, R. & Ranson, S., 'Power and Advantage in Organizations', *Organization Studies*, 2(2), 131–152, 1981.

Wamsley, G. L. & Zald, N. N., 'The Political Economy of Public Organizations', *Public Administration Review*, 33(1), 62–73, 1973.

Wamsley, G. L. & Zald, M. N., *The Political Economy of Public Organizations*, Bloomington, Ind.: Indiana University Press, 1976.

Weber, A. & Taylor, D., 'Procedures for Employee Displacement: Advance Notice of Plant Shutdown', *Journal of Business*, 36(3), 302–315, 1963.

Weiss, C. H. & Bucuvalas, M. J., *Social Science Research and Decision-Making*, New York: Columbia University Press, 1980.

Whyte, T., 'Shutdown: Closing a Plant Is One of the Most Agonizing Jobs a Manager Faces', *Canadian Business*, 55, p. 90, 1982.

Wildavsky, Aaron, *The Politics of the Budgetary Process*, second edition, Boston, Mass.: Little, Brown, 1964.

Winchester, D., 'Industrial Relations Research in Britain', *British Journal of Industrial Relations*, 21, 100–115, 1983.

Zif, J., 'Managerial Strategic Behaviour in State-Owned Enterprises – Business and Political Orientations', *Management Science*, 27(11), 1326–1339, 1981.

Vol. 10

Unemployment: Theory, Policy and Structure

Edited by *Peder J. Pedersen* and *Reinhard Lund*
1987. 15.5 x 23 cm. XX, 358 pages. Cloth. ISBN 3 11 011071 7; 0-89925-277-X (U.S.)

Vol. 11

Organization of Innovation

East-West-Perspectives

Edited by *John Child* and *Paul Bate*
1987. 15.5 x 23 cm. X, 238 pages. Cloth. ISBN 3 11 010700 7; 0-89925-167-6 (U.S.)

Vol. 12

Management in China during and after Mao in Enterprises, Government, and Party

By *Oiva Laaksonen*
1988. 15.5 x 23 cm. X, 379 pages. Cloth. ISBN 3 11 009958 6; 0-89925-025-4 (U.S.)

Vol. 13

Innovation and Management

International Comparisons

Edited by *Kuniyoshi Urabe, John Child* and *Tadao Kagono*
1988. 15.5 x 23 cm. XX, 371 pages. Cloth. ISBN 3 11 011007 5; 0-89925-294-X (U.S.)

Vol. 15

Boards of Directors under Public Ownership:

A Comparative Perspective

By *Miriam Dornstein*
1988. 15.5 x 23 cm. X, 165 pages. Cloth. ISBN 3 11 011740 1; 0-89925-496-9 (U.S.)

Vol. 16

The State, Trade Unions and Self-Management

Issues of Competence and Control

Edited by *György Széll, Paul Blyton,* and *Chris Cornforth*
1989. 15.5 x 23 cm. X, 362 pages. With 11 figures and 8 tables. Cloth. ISBN 3 11 011667 7; 0-89925-475-6 (U.S.)

WALTER DE GRUYTER · BERLIN · NEW YORK
Genthiner Straße 13, D-1000 Berlin 30, Phone (0 30) 2 60 05-0, Telex 1 83 027
200 Saw Mill River Road, Hawthorne, N.Y. 10532, Phone (914) 747-0110, Telex 64 66 77

www.ingramcontent.com/pod-product-compliance
Lightning Source LLC
LaVergne TN
LVHW010549300926
849162LV00002B/274